THE S. S. HUEBNER FOUNDATION
FOR INSURANCE EDUCATION

Studies

THE ECONOMIC THEORY OF RISK
AND INSURANCE

THE S. S. HUEBNER FOUNDATION
FOR INSURANCE EDUCATION

David McCahan, *Editor*

Lectures

LIFE INSURANCE:
TRENDS AND PROBLEMS

THE BENEFICIARY
IN LIFE INSURANCE

LIFE INSURANCE TRENDS
AT MID-CENTURY

Studies

AN ANALYSIS OF
GOVERNMENT LIFE INSURANCE

AN ANALYSIS OF
GROUP LIFE INSURANCE

THE ECONOMIC THEORY OF RISK
AND INSURANCE

THE ECONOMIC THEORY

OF

RISK AND INSURANCE

by

ALLAN H. WILLETT, Ph.D.

Philadelphia
UNIVERSITY OF PENNSYLVANIA PRESS

LONDON: GEOFFREY CUMBERLEGE
OXFORD UNIVERSITY PRESS

1951

HB
601
W6
1951

This book was first published in 1901
By The Columbia University Press as
Volume XIV, Number 2, in *Studies in
History, Economics and Public Law*

THE S. S. HUEBNER FOUNDATION FOR INSURANCE EDUCATION

The S. S. Huebner Foundation for Insurance Education was created in 1940, under the sponsorship of a Cooperating Committee representing the life insurance institution, to aid in strengthening insurance education on the collegiate level. It functions along three principal lines:

1. Providing fellowships and scholarships to aid teachers in accredited colleges and universities of the United States and Canada, or persons who are contemplating a teaching career in such colleges and universities, to secure preparation at the graduate level for insurance teaching and research.
2. Building up and maintaining a research service center in insurance books and other source material which will be available through circulating privileges to teachers in accredited colleges and universities desirous of conducting research in insurance subjects.
3. Publishing research theses and other studies which constitute a distinct contribution directly or indirectly to insurance knowledge.

The activities of the Foundation are under the direction of an Administrative Board consisting of six officers and faculty members of the University of Pennsylvania and two faculty members of other universities.

FOREWORD

This is an unusual volume. It is a reprint—of a doctoral dissertation—originally published in limited quantity just fifty years ago—with copies now virtually unavailable. But its true significance lies not in such facts but in the continuous recognition that its contents have received from insurance educators and economists. As Dr. Robert Riegel, Professor of Statistics and Insurance at the University of Buffalo, said in his letter urging that the Foundation issue this under its imprint, "One of the classic books on Insurance is Allan H. Willett's *The Economic Theory of Risk and Insurance,* published as one of the Columbia Studies in History, Economics and Public Law. This has long been a scarce item, in fact, impossible to buy, although every student of Insurance knows that it was the first and still remains the best discussion of the economic principles of Insurance."

Publication of such a volume is in accord with one of the primary objectives of The S. S. Huebner Foundation for Insurance Education, which is to publish research theses and other studies that constitute a distinct contribution directly or indirectly to insurance knowledge. In conformity with this objective, the Foundation has already undertaken the issuance of two series of volumes, known as "Huebner Foundation Lectures" and "Huebner Foundation Studies," the first series comprising a compilation of addresses on selected insurance topics and the second presenting the results of thorough research in specific areas. In re-publishing Dr. Willett's thesis it seems appropriate to group it with the "Studies" series.

The probability of a volume proving useful to teachers engaged in insurance educational work, especially on the college level, has been a prime consideration in the Foundation's publication policy. Experienced insurance teachers whose views were sought by the Administrative Board on the wisdom of publishing this particular work were unanimous in their conviction that the

Foundation would be rendering a genuine service to insurance teachers and their students in taking such action. But its value to others, such as teachers and students in pure and applied economics, and persons concerned with the broad areas of business organization and management, should not be overlooked. In fact, when comparison is made of the status today of insurance education and of collegiate education for business generally with the relatively small beginnings that had been made along both lines when this dissertation first appeared, it is not inconceivable that its benefits may be more widespread and significant during the half-century to come than in that which has passed.

Dr. Willett, son of a Baptist minister, was born in 1863 at Southwick, Massachusetts. He prepared for college at the Connecticut Literary Institution, from which he entered Brown University where he specialized in Latin and Greek. After his graduation from Brown in 1886, he taught the classics for a number of years in secondary schools and in Urbana University, Urbana, Ohio. A growing interest in the field of economics prompted him to enter Columbia University in 1898 and to study for the doctorate, with particular emphasis upon the economic theory of risk and insurance. He received the degree of Doctor of Philosophy in 1901, submitting the thesis here presented in partial fulfillment of the requirements. From 1901 to 1905, Dr. Willett taught Economics at Brown University and then joined the faculty of the newly established Carnegie Institute of Technology where he later introduced a new branch of technical training known as commercial engineering. During World War I he was engaged in war work in Washington with the Bureau of Labor Statistics but in 1920 became Statistician of the National Coal Association, with which he remained until his retirement in 1939. He now resides in Biloxi, Mississippi. It is interesting to note that Dr. Willett's academic and professional interests have been transmitted to his three sons, Dr. Hurd Curtis Willett, Professor of Meteorology at Massachusetts Institute of Technology, Dr. Edward Francis Willett, Professor of Economics at Smith College, and Merrill Hosmer Willett, Civil Engineer, Metropolitan Board of Transportation, New York City.

Grateful acknowledgment is made to our versatile author and to Columbia University Press for granting to the Foundation

the right of reprinting. It is in nowise a reflection on them to
point out that, although publication of this volume has been
sponsored by the Foundation, the very nature of the purposes
for which the Foundation was created precludes it from taking
an editorial position on controversial theories or practices
relating to insurance.

DAVID McCAHAN

Executive Director

The S. S. Huebner Foundation for

Insurance Education

Philadelphia
September, 1951

PREFACE

The following study deals almost exclusively with the idealized conditions of the static state. It only incidentally attempts to show the bearing of the static laws on the phenomena of the real world or the practices of existing insurance companies. It must consequently wear something of the air of unreality which attaches to all discussions that deal largely with abstractions. Its only purpose is to shed a little light on a rather neglected portion of pure economic theory.

A word of explanation may be in order with regard to my failure to give credit to others in all cases for ideas which have been published before. This has sometimes been due to the fact that the ideas were so much common property that it was impossible to assign them to any particular writer. In other instances the omission is to be explained on the ground that in the course of a considerable amount of reading on the subject of insurance, the significance of many statements was overlooked at the time when they were read. After their importance had come to be appreciated, it was not always possible to trace them to their sources.

It gives me pleasure to acknowledge my indebtedness to my friend, Professor James P. Kelley, for the valuable assistance which he has given me in preparing this book for the press. He kindly undertook to read it all in the proof, and I have been indebted to his suggestions for many improvements, both in substance and in form.

ALLAN H. WILLETT.

Columbia University, May 20, 1901.

CONTENTS

xiii

CONTENTS

CHAPTER III

THE COST OF RISK

CHAPTER IV

THE ASSUMPTION OF RISK

CHAPTER V

THE REWARD FOR RISK-TAKING

CHAPTER VI

WAYS OF MEETING RISK

CONTENTS

CHAPTER VII

INSURANCE

CHAPTER VIII

CONCLUSION

INTRODUCTION

In the present unsettled condition of economic theory and of economic terminology, a profitable discussion of any theoretical question is hardly possible without a preliminary declaration of faith and definition of terms. Much that I have to say about risk and insurance concerns matters of fact, and will be found equally true, or false, under any view of distribution. But it is different with such problems of theory as the economic identity of the risk-taker, or the influence of insurance on distribution. How is it possible to determine the relation of the entrepreneur to risk, before an agreement has been reached as to the function of the entrepreneur and the nature of his reward? How can the place of insurance in economic theory be established, before it has been made clear what are considered to be the correct categories of distribution? There is need of no further justification for prefacing a study of a special subject like insurance with a preliminary statement of the general theory of distribution on which the argument is based, than the desire to avoid ambiguity in the use of terms, and so to assure the meeting of minds which is as essential to an intelligent disagreement among economists as it is to a binding agreement among lawyers.

The theory of distribution on which the following discussion is based, is in all essential respects the *specific productivity* theory elaborated by Professor J. B. Clark, and partially given out in his recent work on *The Distribution of Wealth*. According to that theory there are two, and only two, productive factors, labor and capital. All wealth is the product of these two factors. Under the influence of static forces there is a constant tendency not only to give to each factor as a whole the part of the product whose creation is the result of its presence, but also to give to every unit of labor and to every unit of capital that part of the product that is specifically imputable to it, and to make those specific contributions and rewards to either agent uniform throughout the industrial system. Dynamic forces, on the other hand, are continually introducing new disturbances into the industrial system and creating new variations in the productivity of different units of labor and capital. In the world of reality both kinds of forces are in operation, the latter causing new discrepancies between actual values and normal values, and the former gradually obliterating them after they have been created.

It is no part of my task to attempt a complete statement of the specific productivity theory of distribution, or to enter into a discussion of the arguments for and against it. But there are two points in the theory which must be touched upon in order to make the following discussion intelligible. It is my purpose to attempt to show the influence of risk and of insurance on static rates of wages and interest; and that makes necessary a statement of the relation of risk to the static state. I shall also discuss the connection between the reward for risk-taking and the income of the entrepreneur; and as there is no phase of economic theory which is in a more unsettled condition than the doctrine of the entrepreneur, a preliminary explanation of the conception of his function on which the argument is based seems indispensable.

The Static State

The conception of the static state is purely ideal. Economists have always recognized the necessity of distinguishing between existing values and *normal* or *natural* values, and have made more or less successful attempts to isolate the forces which contribute to the determination of the latter, and to study them apart from temporary and local disturbances. What earlier writers did in a more or less indefinite and incomplete way, Professor Clark has done definitely and completely. He has made a clear and precise distinction between the forces which are responsible for variations of existing values from normal values, and those which are continually tending to bring about agreement between the two. To the latter class of forces he applies the term static; and the static state is one in which all disturbing forces have ceased to act, and actual values have been brought into agreement with normal or *static* values.

The conception of the static state is reached by a process of abstraction. It is necessary in the first place to put aside all economic phenomena which occasion new variations in the productivity of different units of labor and capital.[1] These are caused by dynamic changes, which may be grouped under five heads: changes in the quantity of labor, changes in the quantity of capital, changes in technical methods of production, changes in methods of industrial organization, and changes in human wants.[2] Moreover the process of abstraction cannot stop here. If all dynamic changes were to cease, the ideal static state would never be realized in human society. There are other assumptions which have to be made, such as a high degree of mobility of capital and labor, the universal prevalence of the economic motive,[3] and the power of accurately foreseeing the future. These

[1] Professor Clark in his classification of dynamic changes includes only such as are found in a progressive society. But he recognizes that a complete science of dynamics would have to include a discussion of the effects of changes in the opposite direction, a theory of retrogression as well as a theory of progress.

[2] It has been suggested that changes in legal relations ought to be recognized as a separate group. This would include changes in laws affecting property rights, franchises, taxation, immigration, and the like. Manifestly such changes have a very disturbing effect on economic relations; but it is only in so far as they bring about economic changes. They are primarily social, and all the possible secondary changes of an economic nature are included in the classification given above.

[3] The relation of competition to the static state has been discussed by Mr. Padan in a recent number of the *Journal of Political Economy* (Vol. ix, no. 2, p. 182, *et seq.*). He proposes to include "circumstances of competition" as "an important agent of a highly dynamic character." His idea of the static state involves the absence of competition. According to his conception "a static state is simply an instantaneous photograph of a dynamic period *(sic)* at any moment." Manifestly such a static state "is incapable of setting a standard (of wages and interest) because it is incapable of creating one." The unequal rates of wages and interest brought about by the previous dynamic changes would simply be perpetuated. But it is very different with the static condition here described. If the dynamic changes above enumerated were to cease, there would be a period during which capital and labor would be shifting from group to group, seeking the most advantageous employment. After a time, however, the existing amount of the two agents would be so apportioned that all units of each would be equally productive, and there would no longer be any reason for shifting. Mr. Padan tries to make it appear that we have here two kinds of static state, and that in the former, according to Professor Clark, competition is imperfect, and in the latter perfect, and that perfect competition is no competition. The fact is, of course, that the intermediate condition is not a static state, that the static state is reached only when the condition of uniform productivity prevails, that such a condition would be permanent for lack of any incentive to change, and that competition, or the desire to improve one's economic condition, is assumed to be just as "perfect," that is, "active," in the one state as in the other. In the ideal static state its effect is not seen in motion because there is no advantage to be gained by movement. But to say for that reason that it is absent is as absurd as to say that the force of gravitation is not acting on the water in a pond if there is no motion of the drops.

assumptions depart more or less from the actual condition of things. Labor and capital are far from being absolutely mobile, rates of wages and interest are not determined exclusively by economic considerations, and the result of an industrial operation does not always agree with the expectations of those who enter upon it.

It is the influence of the last of these disturbing factors on static rates of wages and interest that we are to seek to determine. The ideal static adjustment could be realized only on the condition that there were no discrepancies between the anticipated and the actual results of economic activity. Production and consumption must go on either with absolute uniformity or with a regular periodicity which in a series of years would result in uniformity. Unusually warm winters with a reduced consumption of woolens and furs, or unusually dry summers with a reduced production of agricultural commodities, must occur at stated intervals, if at all, so that they may be accurately foreseen and provided for. The unreasoning vagaries of fashion, which cause unexpected shiftings of value from one form of commodity to another, must be replaced by a fixed or a uniformly varying demand, whose effect on values can be anticipated.

While unforeseen losses are occurring, either through the failure of an industrial operation to yield the physical product which it was expected to give, or through a variation between the anticipated and the actual value of the product, the ideal static state is not realized. Every such loss is in itself a dynamic change. The possibility of such chance variations is one of the conditions under which economic activity is carried on. It is a fact of experience to which mankind has to adapt itself, just as it adapts itself to the other conditions of its physical environment. An unexpected loss, when it occurs, reduces the amount of capital at some point in the industrial system, and the failure of an anticipated loss to appear leaves an abnormally large amount of capital in some part of the system. Every occurrence of either kind makes necessary more or less shifting of capital to restore the static condition.

While uncertainty exists, then, the ideal static state can never be realized. Not only do the losses cause a disturbance of the static adjustment, but the risk of loss also has an influence on economic activity. In discussing the pure static theory it is necessary to abstract from the possibility of accidental loss, and to assume a degree of certainty in human affairs which does not actually exist. The purpose of the following discussion is to restore to this conception the element of risk, and to determine in what way the static state, as it can be realized while risk exists, differs from the ideal static state for whose realization the absence of risk must be assumed. If men should acquire no greater control over the forces of nature and no better devices for restraining the irregularities of human conduct, than they now possess, and if knowledge and ability to foresee the future should remain in their present imperfect condition, the static state which would develop even after the lapse of a long period of time could be only approximately perfect. Rates of wages and interest would not exactly coincide with static rates. Why they would vary under the influence of risk, and to what degree, are the questions which we are to try to answer. As a matter of convenience we shall refer to the perfect adjustment which would be reached in the absence of all disturbing forces, including risk itself, as the *ideal static state,* and to the adjustment which would be reached while risk continued to affect human activity, as the *approximate static state.* And we shall first endeavor to discover the effect of the existence of risk unmodified by the influence of any social device for counteracting it, and then see in what way and to what degree the introduction of insurance will modify this influence.

Profit and the Entrepreneur

The only phase of the theory of risk which has been discussed to any extent has concerned the relation which it bears to the function and reward of the entrepreneur. Does the income of the entrepreneur consist in whole or in part of reward for assuming risk? The answer to that question will evidently depend on the definition which is given to the term entrepreneur. It is necessary, then, to state clearly the sense in which the term is used, before attempting to pass judgment upon the connection of the entrepreneur with risk and the reward for assuming it.

There are two ways of approaching the problem of the entrepreneur. We may seek to determine what forms of activity he carries on, and from them infer under which of the categories of distribution his income falls; or we may differentiate the various forms of economic income, and identify the entrepreneur by the fact that he receives a distinct share in the distributive process. The problem is usually approached from the side of activity, and not of reward. The attempt is made to identify the entrepreneur by considering what he does, and not what he receives. He is regarded as the captain who marshals and directs the productive forces of society. He brings together labor and capital, to co-operate in the production of the commodities which society needs. He strives to anticipate future changes in human wants, and to adapt the stream of commodities to the demands of society. He is perpetually on the alert to devise improvements in organization or in methods of production which will diminish his expenses, and to adopt such improvements when introduced by others. It is the activity of entrepreneurs which is continually causing divergences between expense of production and price, and it is the competition of entrepreneurs which tends to annihilate these divergences after they have appeared, and in the end to assure to capitalists and laborers the entire product of their industry.

Under which category of economic activity does this service of directing the productive forces of society fall? On this question there appears the greatest diversity of opinion. To some the person who renders it is a laborer, performing a special kind of work, and his income appears as wages of management; to others he is a capitalist, serving society by carrying risk, and his reward, though called by another name, is a form of interest; while still others look upon him as a combination of laborer and capitalist, and consider his extra gain to be due to the advantage this dual role assures him.

This very diversity of opinion is an indication of the complexity of the service which the captain of industry renders. He is undoubtedly a laborer, and it is necessary to recognize in his income an element of wages. Its amount would be determined in the same way as the wages of any independent workman are determined. It is that part of his income which he could obtain by giving the service of his knowledge and ability to an employer. He may be a capitalist, and if he is, his income contains an element of interest, which is equal in amount to the return he could obtain by allowing another person to use his capital. He may be the residual claimant in the industry which he directs, and as such he will receive the profit of the industry, the residual product after allowing for the payment of all labor and capital employed, his own included.

Now in the accepted nomenclature of economic science, the term entrepreneur has come to designate this director of industry. But it is evident that such a conception is extremely complex, involving more than one of the distinct forms of economic activity. It is consequently of little service in attempts to solve problems of distribution. The chief reason for differentiating the entrepreneur from the other productive agents is the desire to dispose of the element in distribution which is neither wages nor interest, and which is commonly called profit. In other words, the conception of the entrepreneur which will be useful in economic analysis is the one which is obtained by approaching the problem from the side of reward instead of that of activity.

All wealth is produced by capital and labor. In an ideal static state the productivity of all units of capital is the same, and each unit receives as its share in the distributive process the portion of the product specifically attributable to it. The same thing is true of labor. Interest, the return to capital, and wages, the return to labor, absorb the entire net product of industry. But in a dynamic state this uniformity of productivity does not prevail. Dynamic changes are continually disturbing the static adjustment. An improvement in technique, for example, introduced in a particular factory belonging to a special industry, reduces the expense of producing the commodity which the factory turns out. So long as this factory has a monopoly of the improvement, it may continue to sell its output at the price fixed by the former cost of production. The same amount of product can be turned out with a smaller amount of capital and labor, or a larger amount of product with the same amount of capital and labor. That is, the productivity of each unit of labor and capital in the group is increased. The excess of receipts over expenses of production, with market wages for labor and interest for capital included in the latter, is profit. Its source is usually in a dynamic change, resulting in a localized lowering of expense of production, or, what is the same thing, in a localized increase in the productivity of capital and labor.

It is clear that under free competition such a profit must always be transient; it can endure only while the monopoly endures. As other factories adopt the same improvement, the supply of goods at the lower cost of production is increased, until finally the entire demand is supplied at the reduced cost and the price drops to the level which the new cost justifies. When that point is reached, if we disregard secondary changes induced by the primary one, the gain from the improved method of production, which at first appeared as a profit in a particular part of the industrial system, has become a permanent net addition to the productivity of all capital and labor, through the fall in the price of the commodity.

It is clear, therefore, why profit may properly be called a dynamic income. If all dynamic changes were to cease, unequal rates of productivity of capital and labor in different parts of the industrial system would result in a shifting of capital and labor from less productive to more productive groups, until a uniform rate of productivity had finally been reached. The profit would endure only so long as the influence of the dynamic change was felt; with the attainment of the perfect static adjustment it would entirely disappear.

Profit, then, appears as a result of the abnormal productivity of capital and labor in some part of the industrial system. Like all abnormal gains, it is due to a monopoly advantage. But it by no means follows that all monopoly gains ought to be classed as profit. Profit has to be distinguished from certain permanent monopoly gains which either capital or labor individually may create, and which they are, therefore, able to retain as their own income. If certain laborers are in a position to prevent the free flow of labor into their industry and so to keep up the marginal productivity of labor in it, they may be at the same time in a position to force from the employers, in the form of higher wages, the entire excess product; and in the same way, if certain capitalists have a similar monopoly power, they can appropriate to themselves the resulting monopoly gain. If, however, the restriction on the flow of capital into the industry is due to the power of the entrepreneur to keep it out, as in the case of his ownership of a patent-right, the resulting abnormal product is an entrepreneur's profit. Profit is due to the increased productivity of the industry as a whole. Laborers as such have no claim to it, as they are entitled to no more than the market rate of wages; capitalists as such cannot appropriate it, as their reward is determined by the market rate of interest. The monopoly gains of labor alone or of capital alone are created by the agents which receive them; profit is an extra product, created by capital and labor as the result of a localized increase of productivity, which neither is in a strategic position to claim for itself.

It is profit as thus defined which Professor Clark regards as the peculiar reward of the entrepreneur. Considered from the side of his income, the entrepreneur is a person who is in a position to appropriate the results of the extra productivity of capital and labor. The person to whom such extra gains accrue in any industry is the person who has the legal right to the residual product of the industry. Cases can be imagined in which they would accrue to one who had contributed neither capital nor labor. Such a person would be a *pure entrepreneur,* and his income would be *pure profit.* But it is evident that generally speaking the residual claimant or entrepreneur is at the same time a capitalist. He owns the whole or a part of the capital invested in the industry, and his claim to the residual share of the product is based on his property rights. Such a person combines the functions of capitalist and entrepreneur, and only that part of his income is profit which is in excess of the return he could obtain by allowing another to use his capital in the same way in which he is himself using it.

Such is the conception of the function and reward of the entrepreneur which is obtained by considering them from the side of income. The residual claimant in any industry is the entrepreneur. Evidently it is impossible to reconcile this conception with the popular one described above. If the same term is to be employed to denote the person who is entitled to the residual share of the product, called profit, and the person who renders the complex industrial service commonly attributed to the entrepreneur, it is necessary to show, first, that there are no directors of industry who are not residual claimants, and, second, that there are no residual claimants who are not directors of industry. Neither of these claims can be established unless we give to the term *director of industry* a much broader meaning than it has in popular usage. The owner of a few shares of stock in a large corporation is one of the residual claimants, entitled to a portion of any profit which may appear; but common economic usage hardly justifies us in calling him an entrepreneur. It is true that he is legally entitled to a voice in controlling the policy of the corporation through his right to vote for the board of directors; but such imperfect and remote control as that is not the form which is had in mind when the director of industry is spoken of. On the other hand, the work of directing the productive forces of society is often done by men whose income is entirely in the form of a fixed salary. Hired managers are frequently the ones who inaugurate improvements in any industry or adopt improvements introduced by others, and help to establish the productivity rate of wages and interest, which is one of the chief results of the activity of the directors of industry. Common usage does not justify us in denying to such a person the title of entrepreneur.

If the preceding analysis is correct, it is impossible to establish any necessary and universal connection between the one who performs the function of the entrepreneur, as the term is ordinarily used, and the recipient of the residual product of industry called profit. A recognition of these facts will clear up many of the difficulties which have arisen from the attempt to use the same term to denote the two persons. Common custom has undoubtedly been on the side of using the word to denote the person performing the directive work of society. But, as we have already stated, in discussing questions of distribution it is more useful to adopt a conception of the entrepreneur which connects him with a distinct form of income, than one which is based on a complex form of activity, with no definite significance for distribution.[4] Functional distribution must logically precede personal; and for the purpose of a discussion of functional distribution terms must be defined in such a way that each economic agent may be connected with a distinct form of income. The conception of the entrepreneur as the recipient of the normal profit must be acknowledged to be more precise and more serviceable than the complex conception commonly attributed to the term.

[4] The entrepreneur has a certain function, but it is of a passive, mercantile nature, not to be confounded with the active function of the captain of industry. I have placed a great deal of emphasis upon the income, because it is easier to identify the entrepreneur by means of it than in any other way.

It is customary in economic analysis to speak of capitalists and laborers as though they were always separate and distinct persons. It is just as convenient many times to use the conception of a *pure entrepreneur,* a man who is neither capitalist nor laborer, and whose income includes neither wages nor interest. It is necessary to think of him as a person who has no capital of his own, but is able in some way to obtain capital from others by paying the market rate of interest; who performs no labor on his own part, but hires the labor of others at the market rate of wages; to whom the product of the industry in the first instance belongs, and whose income is pure profit, the net return which he can obtain for his product in excess of the wages and interest that he has to pay for his labor and capital. In the discussion which follows the term pure entrepreneur is always to be understood in this sense.

The pure entrepreneur with no capital of his own would be at a great disadvantage in the actual world. There are few owners of capital who would be willing to give the use of it to persons with no security to offer for its safe return. The more common form of entrepreneur is one who has some capital of his own which serves as a guarantee fund and enables him to obtain more capital from others. To such a person Professor Clark has given the compound title *capitalist-entrepreneur.*[5] I shall use that term to denote a person who employs his own capital and that of others in the production of commodities, who is the original owner of the product of the industry, and whose income consists of interest on his own capital and whatever net profit may be realized in the sale of the product. Whether speaking of the pure entrepreneur or of the capitalist-entrepreneur as above defined, I shall for the most part leave out of consideration that portion of his income which is attributable to his own labor and which would properly be classed as wages. A pure entrepreneur is one who is entrepreneur and nothing else, and whose income is normal profit; a capitalist-entrepreneur is one who is entrepreneur and capitalist, and whose income consists of interest and profit. And

[5] This term atones by its definiteness for its lack of brevity. President Hadley has used the term *speculator* with much the same meaning, but this word is used in too many other senses to be very precise. Its indefiniteness is probably partly responsible for the large but vague part which risk plays in his theory of distribution.

while, as has been shown, there is no necessary and universal connection between the recipient of profit and the captain of industry, still it may be said that in general it is the entrepreneur as here defined, who performs the directive work of society. It is his desire to realize a profit by lowering the cost of producing commodities which is the main incentive to industrial progress.

THE ECONOMIC THEORY OF
RISK AND INSURANCE

CHAPTER I

THE NATURE OF RISK

To live and labor in uncertainty is the common lot of all men. Life and health, property and income, are all exposed to countless dangers. The precariousness of the results of human effort has been a favorite theme of poets and philosophers of all ages. "The best laid schemes o' mice an' men Gang aft agley," and the possibility of such a mischance profoundly modifies the conduct of rational beings. In their economic activity in particular the influence of uncertainty can be clearly discerned. While exact mathematical measurements are in the nature of the case impossible, the direction of this influence, and to an approximate extent its degree, may be ascertained. It has long been considered a commonplace of economic theory that the reward of capital, and to a less extent the reward of labor, varies directly as the degree of risk to which they are exposed as a result of their economic activity. But until recently, no attempt has been made to isolate the phenomena of risk and risk-taking, and to determine the laws which govern them. The new interest in the subject has sprung for the most part from discussions as to the exact nature of the function and reward of the entrepreneur. Professor Mangoldt in Germany, and Mr. Hawley in the United States, have made independent attempts to elaborate a theory of distribution in which the assumption of certain risks shall be the special function of the entrepreneur, and his income the reward for risk-taking; and though few writers have adopted their general doctrine, the notion that in some way the function of the entrepreneur has a peculiar connection with risk is by no means uncommon. In all the previous discussion, however, one will search in vain for a thorough treatment of the nature of economic risk and the way in which its influence makes itself felt.

We are told by the philosophers that all the activities of the universe are obedient to law. Nowhere have they left any opportunity for the intrusion of chance. Events which appear to take place in a purely accidental way are just as much determined as those whose occurrence can be accurately foretold. The appearance of accident is due entirely to human limitations. It is because we do not know all the previous conditions or all the laws governing them that a particular phenomenon appears to us to occur by chance. In this sense, then, chance is purely subjective; it is merely an appearance, resulting from the imperfection of man's knowledge, and not a part of the course of external nature. But the term may be used also in an objective sense. By chance in that sense is meant the degree of probability that a particular event will occur, as it is estimated with the aid of all the attainable knowledge of the preceding conditions. If the only fact known about the condition of a number of balls in a bottle is that there is an equal number of white ones and of black ones, there is an even chance that the first ball to come out will be white, and this chance is independent of any personal peculiarities of the person who estimates it. It is in this objective sense that the term is commonly used, and, to avoid any possibility of ambiguity, it is in this sense alone that it will be used in the following pages. By chance will be meant the degree of probability of the occurrence of any future event.[1] It may vary all the way from absolute certainty that an event will not occur, through the different degrees of probability, to absolute certainty that it will occur.

Chance affects economic activity through the psychological influence of uncertainty. Man's conduct is modified in one way by coming events which he can definitely foresee and provide for, though he can do nothing to prevent their occurrence; it is affected in a different way by events which are only possible, and which may never occur, or may occur at an unexpected time. In the latter case he will not act just as he would if he knew that they would occur, and occur at a definite time, and he will not act just as he would if he knew they would not occur at all. His conduct will be modified by the very uncertainty as to the occurrence of the future event, that is, by what appears to him as chance.

A distinction must be made and kept clearly in mind between

[1] This term may also be used to denote the probability that an event has occurred in the past, when it is impossible to obtain any certain information about it. Premiums for the insurance of overdue ships are determined partly by the chance of loss as estimated from past experience.

the chance, or the degree of probability, and the degree of uncertainty. Manifestly the greatest degree of uncertainty does not accompany the greatest degree of probability. When the chance is zero, the uncertainty is also zero. A slight degree of probability brings with it a slight degree of uncertainty. But the two cannot go on indefinitely increasing at the same rate, as at the end of the series we should have the absurd combination of the highest degree of probability, which is certainty, with the highest degree of uncertainty. The uncertainty is the greatest when the chances are even, that is, when the degree of probability is represented by the fraction $\frac{1}{2}$. In such a case we say that there is nothing to show what the outcome will be. As we go from an even chance either towards greater probability or towards less probability, the uncertainty diminishes, and at either end of the series it entirely disappears. For example, there is an even chance that the first card drawn from a perfect pack will be red or black, and there is absolute uncertainty as to which it will be. If, however, one of the red suits is replaced by a third black suit, the degree of probability is altered. The chance of drawing a red card is now one in four, and the chance of drawing a black one is three in four. The chance has been increased or decreased, according to the color whose appearance is made the basis of comparison. But the degree of uncertainty has been reduced, and this is equally true of the uncertainty about the appearance of either color. And after a black suit has been substituted for the remaining red suit, the chance of drawing a red card has been reduced to zero, and the chance of drawing a black card has been increased to a hundred per cent, while all uncertainty as to which color will be drawn has disappeared.

I have dwelt at such length upon this simple distinction because of its fundamental importance for the determination of the nature of risk. The word risk, as it is employed in common speech, is by no means free from ambiguity. It is sometimes used in a subjective sense to denote the act of taking a chance, but more commonly and preferably in an objective sense to denote some condition of the external world. To avoid ambiguity its use in the following pages will be confined to this latter sense. The act of incurring a risk will be called risk-taking or the assumption of risk.

But even when used in this objective sense its significance is

not always the same. It is possible to think of risk either in relation to probability or in relation to uncertainty. As the degree
of probability of loss increases from zero to one hundred per
cent, the degree of risk may be said to increase *pari passu*. This
is undoubtedly the way in which the term is ordinarily used. A
person who should enter upon an undertaking in which the
chances were ninety in a hundred that it would result in failure,
would undoubtedly be said to run a tremendous risk. But if the
term is used in this sense, it will not be true, as I shall attempt
to show later on, that the special net reward for assuming risk
invariably increases as the degree of risk increases. This net premium increases as the uncertainty increases; but after the point
of even chances is passed, the uncertainty diminishes as the
probability increases. Beyond that point, therefore, the net
premium for risk-taking will also diminish as the probability of
the occurrence of the loss increases. When the loss is certain to
occur the premium entirely disappears, as in the case of the
ordinary replacement of capital used up in productive operations.
As, however, the risks assumed in industrial life are usually well
below the point of even chances, so that the uncertainty as to the
outcome increases as the probability of loss increases, it will be
more convenient to continue the discussion as though such risks
only were to be considered. Whatever statements are intended to
apply to greater chances will be put in a form that will make
their application clear.

This is not the place to undertake to establish the law laid
down above. My only reason for mentioning it here is to show
why it seems necessary to define risk with reference to the degree
of uncertainty about the occurrence of a loss, and not with reference to the degree of probability that it will occur. Risk in this
sense is the objective correlative of the subjective uncertainty. It
is the uncertainty considered as embodied in the course of events
in the external world, of which the subjective uncertainty is a
more or less faithful interpretation.[2]

[2] This definition involves considerable departure from ordinary usage. The
word *uncertainty* might be used in this objective sense, or a new term might
be coined to designate its objective aspect. But it has seemed better to keep
to the term ordinarily used by economists in this connection. It is important
not only to develop more clearly than has yet been done the effect of risk on
economic activity, but also to note that many of the statements commonly
made about it are true only when the term is defined in this way.

Considering risk in this sense, we find that the method by which the degree of risk may be ascertained depends upon the relative perfection of the knowledge of preceding conditions. In some cases it may be known directly from the circumstances attending it. The uncertainty about the color of a card drawn at random from a perfect pack is of this kind. No one would consider that the chance at the tenth trial was altered by the fact that at every one of the preceding nine trials a red card had been drawn. But when no such definite knowledge of preceding conditions is attainable, the degree of risk is estimated in a different way. It is ascertained by applying the laws of probability to the accumulated results of past experience. The chance that a particular loss will occur is denoted by the fraction expressing the ratio between the actual number of such losses and the possible number in a given period of time. If during each year for a series of years the loss has been one in one hundred in the case of buildings of a certain kind, the chance that a similar building will be destroyed during the following year is expressed by the fraction $\frac{1}{100}$ on condition that there is no appreciable change in the methods adopted for preventing loss. If for the moment we assume that it is known that the actual number of losses every year will correspond with the average number, the only uncertainty for the group as a whole will be as to which of the buildings will be the one to suffer the loss. The chance that any particular building will be destroyed will be one in a hundred, but the number of losses for the group as a whole will be fixed.

But as a matter of fact the loss for the group as a whole is not likely to correspond exactly with the average loss as determined by past experience. The actual number of losses in any year will vary more or less from the average. This variation is not absolutely indefinite. By the laws of chance a figure can be obtained which will indicate the probable variation of the actual number of losses from the average. This figure will vary in different cases according to the nature of the series from which the average has been obtained. The probable variation will be much less in the case of a series in which the losses from year to year have varied little from the average, than it will be in the case of a series which shows great fluctuations. Thus, to take a simple illustration, if the losses for four years have been 1, 11, 30 and 18 per hundred, the average is 15 per hundred, but it is evident that the actual number may vary greatly from the average. If on the other hand the series had been 13, 14, 16 and 17, while the average would have been the same as before, the actual number for the following year would be much more likely to be near the average. The probable variation of the actual number of losses from the average may be ascertained by calculating the average of the actual variations during the series of years under observation. Thus in the first illustration given above, the variations were respectively 14, 4, 15 and 3, giving an average variation of 9. In the second series the variations were 2, 1, 1 and 2, and the average was 1½. It is evident, therefore, that the greater the fluctuations are from year to year in the number of losses, the greater is the uncertainty as to the number which will occur in a particular year. It must be borne in mind that risk is connected with the uncertainty. If the number of losses may vary from 1 to 30, the area of uncertainty includes the entire number of possible losses; but if the number may vary only from 13 to 17, then whatever may be the uncertainty about the fate of any particular building, for the group as a whole 13 losses can be counted upon, and the area of uncertainty includes only the 5 losses from the 13th to the 17th.

This distinction between the certain and the uncertain losses is of the utmost importance. If, as I shall attempt to show, uncertainty imposes a cost upon society, the removal of the uncertainty will in itself be a source of gain—not that the replacement of the possibility of a small amount of loss by the certainty of a large amount would result in a net gain. The effect of the occurrence of disaster is in itself the same, whether it was foreseen or not. It is the destruction of a certain amount of capital. But the net result of the occurrence of a certain amount of loss which was definitely foreseen, is different from the net result of the occurrence of the same amount of loss, plus previous uncertainty whether it would be greater or smaller. And the influence of the latter element is greater when the anticipation of future loss is based on an average obtained from a fluctuating series of past losses. The greater the probable variation of the actual loss from the average, the greater the degree of uncertainty.

Finally it must be noted that the probable variation varies

with the number of cases included in a group. According to the well-known statistical law, the figure denoting the probable variation increases only as the square root of the number of cases. Increasing the number of similar risks a hundredfold increases the probable variation by only tenfold. If for example we assume that past experience, based on the observation of 10,000 cases for a number of years, has shown that on the average one house in every thousand is destroyed by fire each year, the average loss has been 10 houses a year. But the actual loss has varied from year to year. The probable variation of the actual loss from the average can be determined only by a calculation based on the actual losses during the years under observation. But we will assume that for 10,000 cases this variation is 5. Then if there is no change in the chance of destruction to which the houses are exposed, the loss next year will probably be between 5 and 15. It is probable that as many as 5 and no more than 15 of the houses will burn. The area of uncertainty, then, is 10, or 1/10 of 1 per cent of the number of cases. If we now increase the number of houses exposed to the same danger a hundredfold, from 10,000 to 1,000,000, the average loss will be 1,000, but the probable variation of the actual loss from the average will not increase a hundredfold, from 5 to 500, but only tenfold, from 5 to 50. The actual loss next year will probably be between 950 and 1050. The area of uncertainty is now 100, or 1/100 of 1 per cent of the number of cases. We have used the term *area of uncertainty* to denote the number of cases lying between the largest probable number of losses, or the average plus the probable variation, and the smallest probable number, or the average minus the probable variation.[3] We may say then that the area of uncertainty increases as the square root of the number of cases, and that its ratio to the entire number of cases becomes correspondingly less.

Risk, in the sense in which we are to use the term, is, so to speak, the objectified uncertainty as to the occurrence of an

3 I need not point out that the average variation itself denotes only a probability and not a certainty. There is additional uncertainty as to the extent to which the actual variation in any year will vary from the probable. I have not thought it necessary to consider the various devices of the mathematicians for obtaining more significant figures than averages. My only purpose is to show that with the increase in the number of cases the actual degree of uncertainty for the entire group diminishes, and that fact is sufficiently well brought out by the use of crude averages.

undesired event. It varies with the uncertainty and not with the degree of probability. In that sense the degree of risk in any individual case is a definite quantity. It may be ascertained in some cases by direct observation of the conditions on which the possibility of the occurrence of the event depends. When such knowledge can not be obtained directly, it is sought indirectly by a statistical study of the results of past experience. The chance of the occurrence of a loss is denoted by the fraction expressing the ratio between the actual number of losses and the possible number in a given period of time. The value of this figure varies with the regularity of the series from which it has been obtained. There is greater uncertainty about the number of losses that will occur in a given year when the average has been obtained from a fluctuating series than when it has been obtained from one which was comparatively uniform. The figure expressing the average variation of the actual losses from the average loss for a number of years is called the probable variation. The greater the ratio between the probable variation and the whole number of cases, the greater is the uncertainty. The probable variation increases only as the square root of the number of cases, therefore its ratio to the whole number becomes less as the number is increased. Consequently the more individual cases there are included in a group, the less is the uncertainty as to the amount of loss which the group as a whole will suffer. The bearing of these laws upon economic conduct, and their significance for economic theory, will appear in subsequent chapters.

CHAPTER II

CLASSES OF RISKS

CAPITAL of any kind is exposed to a certain liability of loss, but the degree of risk varies greatly in different forms of investment. In the same way participation in any form of industrial activity may bring with it some chance of personal injury, but the degree of danger is not the same in all occupations. The minimum degree of risk incurred by the choice of capital goods rather than consumption goods, or by using one's power in any kind of work, does not have the same kind of influence on economic activity as the additional risk involved in particular employments. The former affects directly the willingness of men to labor or to accumulate capital; the latter affects their choice of the manner in which they shall employ their labor or capital.[1] These two kinds of risk may be called *economic,* because their existence is due to participation in economic life.

There are other risks to which men are exposed, the existence of which is not the result of economic activity. In contrast to the former kind these may be called *extra-economic.* Of this kind is the danger of contracting a contagious disease, to which all men are more or less exposed, or the possibility of the loss of consumption goods by fire or theft. Such risks may affect economic activity; but not in the same way as those will affect it which are incurred as an incident of the activity itself. It is one question how a man will act because he is exposed to a certain degree of risk; it is a different question how he will act when the degree of risk depends on his conduct. It is with economic risk alone that we shall be

---

1 Cf. Haynes: "Risk an Economic Factor," *Quarterly Journal of Economics,* vol. ix, p. 410. Mr. Haynes regards the minimum degree of risk to which all capital is exposed as ineffective. Such an adjective, however, can hardly be applied to it. It is certainly "effective," but its effect is not of the same sort as that of the additional risk involved in some investments.

concerned; that is, with the risk that a man incurs on account of his participation in economic life.[2]

If the subjective value which a person puts upon any commodity is higher than its objective exchange value, the loss of the commodity will cause a greater feeling of discomfort than would be occasioned by the loss of an equally costly article, to which no sentimental value attached. It is in general to consumption goods that such abnormal values belong. Souvenirs and heirlooms whose market value is slight may be prized very highly by their possessors on account of their past associations. A particular book or article of furniture may become so necessary to the comfort of its owner that the loss of it will affect him like the departure of a familiar friend. Occasionally the same sort of personal attachment may spring up towards some capital good, as the boat used for a long time by a fisherman, or the building in which a man's business life has been spent. The loss of such a commodity causes a certain amount of personal suffering which is not relieved by the recovery of its market value; and the risk of losing it will have a greater influence than the risk of losing an indifferent commodity of equal value. To this possibility of undergoing personal suffering through the loss of any commodity may be given the name *personal risk*. It is so rarely that its influence is felt in the case of capital goods that it will not be necessary to consider it in discussing the risk to capital. A capitalist is nearly always indifferent about the loss of capital goods of any kind, if he is certain that the full value of the lost property will be restored to him. In most of the risks which he assumes this personal element is entirely lacking.

It is very different with many of the dangers to which the laborer is exposed. The economic risk which threatens him is loss of income. This may be brought about in various ways. Sometimes it is attended with great physical suffering, as when a painful accident incapacitates him for labor; sometimes it brings with it freedom from the necessity of toil, as when it is due to the impossi-

2 It is conceivable that there may be a diminution of risk instead of an increase, as a result of economic activity. Thus wealth invested in government bonds is exposed to less danger than wealth in the form of high-priced driving-horses kept for pleasure. In such cases the opportunity of avoiding risk will have an influence precisely the opposite of that exerted by the necessity of incurring greater risk; but they occur so rarely that they need not be considered in a general discussion.

bility of obtaining employment. In neither case will the certainty of obtaining an income equal to the one he was receiving make the laborer indifferent to the possibility of the occurrence of the event. He will not be willing to endure the physical suffering resulting from the accident, just because his income will be continued; and he will be more than willing to give up the search for employment, if he can obtain as large an income without work as with it.

We have here an important distinction between the dangers which threaten labor and those to which capital is subjected. In nearly all the dangers to which labor is exposed, there is involved a considerable share of what I have called the personal element, while the dangers threatening capital are almost entirely free from it. This fundamental distinction brings with it others no less important, relating to the possibility of transferring risk, and the effect which this possibility has on the conduct of the person who makes the transfer. For that reason it seems inadvisable to attempt to deal with the two kinds of risk in the same discussion. In the following pages we are concerned almost exclusively with risks to capital. Whenever it seems necessary to make any statements about the relation of labor to risk, they will be expressed in such a way as to indicate the class of risks to which they apply.

Risks to capital may be classified in various ways from different points of view and for different purposes. A classification which is of great importance for the technique of insurance is based on the nature of the uncertainty. There may be uncertainty whether the event will occur, when it will take place, or in what way—*casus incertus an, quando,* or *quomodo.* Thus, with reference to a particular building, there is uncertainty whether it will ever be destroyed, when its destruction will occur, and whether it will be due to fire or flood, wind or lightning. The greater the number of these kinds of risk involved in a given case, the greater is the resulting uncertainty. Insurance companies usually limit their responsibility to losses occurring within a fixed time, and in one or more specified ways.

A second form of classification is based on the character of the possible loss. There is the possibility that existing wealth may be lost by its owner, and the possibility that expected future wealth may never be obtained. We may distinguish these forms of loss as positive and negative. The destruction of a building by fire illustrates the former kind; the failure to find the expected market for a commodity is an example of the latter. This classification is of importance for the theory of risk, since the peculiar form of loss caused by uncertainty is entirely of the negative kind. Writers on insurance have had in mind much the same distinction in their recognition of the difference between present and future values. To a certain extent also it corresponds to the distinction between loss of capital and loss of income from capital.

A more fundamental and significant classification of risks than any yet noted is based on the distinction between static and dynamic losses. We have already spoken of the difference between static forces and dynamic forces, and have shown that the conception of the ideal static state, with an absolutely unchanging amount of capital apportioned in such a way as to be uniformly productive, is inconsistent with the existence of risk. For risk involves the possibility of a divergence between the expected course of events and the course actually realized; and every such divergence will result in a change either in the amount of capital or in its apportionment, and so in a disturbance of the static adjustment. The non-occurrence of an expected loss will have this disturbing effect as well as the occurrence of an unexpected loss. In this sense, therefore, the expression *static risk* involves a contradiction of terms.

But we may conceive of a static state of a modified form, which shall embrace the element of uncertainty from which man's economic life can never be free. In this approximate static state certain forms of risk, that is, the possibility of certain forms of accidental loss, will still survive. These risks may be called static, because their existence does not depend upon the occurrence of dynamic changes.[3] They are connected with losses caused by the irregular action of the forces of nature or the mistakes and misdeeds of human beings. According to the occasion of the loss, they may be further subdivided. Some are caused by inanimate forces, as fire, wind, or water; others by the action of animal or plant life,

---

[3] A slight amount of dynamic risk would also be present so long as there were slight local changes in the amount of capital, due to the failure of the actual course of events to agree with the expected course. Every such minute dynamic change would slightly affect values in other parts of the economic system.

as moth or mould; others by the carelessness either of the owner of the wealth destroyed or of another person, which gives opportunity for the unfavorable action of animate or inanimate nature; and still others by the fraud or violence of the criminally disposed, seeking to appropriate to their own use wealth which does not belong to them. All these forms of loss will continue while human life endures, and uncertainty as to the exact time or amount of loss to be anticipated from these sources involves also the existence of static risk.

Dynamic risks are those involved in the possibility of dynamic changes. Not all dynamic changes, however, are equally important in this connection; for it is not the change itself which constitutes the risk, but the uncertainty about the time or amount of future changes. Growth of population and increase of capital take place with comparative regularity, and therefore cause little incidental loss, except in so far as they may be necessary to one of the other dynamic changes, and pave the way for it. It is with changes in human wants, and still more with improvements in machinery and organization, that the greatest amount of uncertainty is connected.[4] Those included in the first of these groups originate on the side of consumption; those in the second, on that of production. To some extent the former are capable of being anticipated or even controlled, while the latter occur in the most irregular and uncertain ways, and to that extent there is greater risk connected with the latter than with the former. No one thing is more essential for success in modern business than the ability to forecast future changes in the desires of consumers. It is important to note also that the loss may result from the non-occurrence of an anticipated event, as well as from the occurrence of one which was not anticipated; and that the special cost entailed upon society by the existence of risk will have to be borne whether or not the uncertain loss actually occurs.

[4] Certain short-time fluctuations in human wants would exist even in the static state. With change of season would come changes in the consumption of commodities; and exceptional events, such as the death of a ruler and the consequent general assumption of mourning, would cause temporary alterations in the character of the articles demanded. So far as these fluctuations occurred with uniform regularity, they could be provided for with accuracy and would involve no risk. So far as the time of their occurrence and the extent of the change could not be foreseen, the possibility of such changes would be a form of static risk.

Examples of the losses caused by these dynamic changes are to be found on every hand. The tide of fashionable travel turns from seashore to mountains, and large investments of capital at ocean resorts lose their value. Bicycles and automobiles are used by people who formerly wanted horses and carriages, and the value of the latter declines. An unexpected change in the fashionable color leaves manufacturers and dealers with stocks of goods which they are obliged to sell at reduced prices. The effect of improvements in mechanical and chemical appliances is equally obvious. A system of street railways operated by cable was introduced in a western city, and when its career of usefulness had hardly begun, it was replaced at great expense by a system operated by electricity. A flouring mill was fitted up with the best available machinery, and within a very short time the new machinery was discarded, and an improved pattern introduced at an expense of hundreds of thousands of dollars. Every investment of capital in forms whose usefulness is limited to the production of a specific commodity, is exposed to the danger of losing its value through discoveries or inventions which render it obsolete and useless.

There is a special form of dynamic risk which needs to be pointed out, both on account of the large part it plays in modern industrial life and because of its great theoretical importance. In a state of society like the present, in which wealth is increasing at a rate out of proportion to the increase in population, there is always a large fund of newly created capital looking for favorable investment. This must be used either in increasing the supply of existing consumption goods or in creating kinds not before produced. These results may be reached either through the larger employment of the kinds of capital goods already in use, or through the creation of new kinds adapted to the production of the old or the new consumption goods. If the only investment for the new capital were to be found in the creation of consumption goods already in use, by methods and machinery now employed, the rate of interest would rapidly fall, and there would be little opportunity for the realization of profit. To avoid this result capital is continually seeking new forms of investment. The simplest device is to invent a cheaper method of creating a commodity already in use. Every improvement of this kind will yield a temporary profit to the entrepreneur who first employs it, but in the end it must result in a lower rate of interest on all capital. As a second resource additional capital goods of forms already employed may be used to create new kinds of consumption goods; or, finally, the new capital may be embodied in new kinds of capital goods, intended for the production of consumption goods not before created. If the new consumption goods produced in either way is one which men desire, so that as a result of its production there is a net increase in the sum of human wants, its influence will be felt in the direction of a greater willingness of men to labor, a consequent greater demand for capital, and a retardation in the fall in the rate of interest. The introduction of the new goods and new machinery also offers an opportunity for the realization of temporary profit by those who first produce or use them.

The relation of risk to these different forms of investment of new capital is readily seen. In the first case no uncertainty is involved, except possibly as to the elasticity of the demand for the commodity whose production is increased. In the second case there is to be added uncertainty as to the technical result, a form of uncertainty which is usually connected to a greater or less extent with the introduction of any untried appliance or process. With the progress of physical science, however, it is evident that this form of uncertainty is being gradually eliminated, and that in many cases the successful working of the new device can be safely counted upon in advance. There is still greater uncertainty involved in the creation of new commodities and new machinery for producing them. If the new commodity is intended to satisfy an existing need, it may be uncertain how far it will accomplish its purpose. The claim that it meets a long felt want is hardly sufficient to assure its success. If, on the other hand, the commodity precedes the want, and is produced with the expectation that its own intrinsic merits and extensive advertising will create a market for it, the possibility of failure is evidently greatly increased. Finally, if existing kinds of capital goods are used in producing a new commodity which fails to find a sale, they can be turned to the employment for which similar machines had been used before and thus preserve a part of their value; but if new kinds of machines have to be brought into service, besides the element of uncertainty as to the technical success of the machine, there is a possibility that the entire investment will be lost if the commodity falls dead on the market.

The investment of capital in attempts to produce new commodities which shall find a ready sale is one of the most characteristic features of modern industrial life. The rapid accumulation of capital, the consequent fall of the rate of interest in old forms of investment, and the large gains to be realized under our patent system by the creation of a new commodity which appeals to the public taste, combine to push production out tentatively in all directions. Large amounts of capital are sunk every year in experiments which end disastrously, and large fortunes are made out of successful ventures. In order to be able to refer without circumlocution to the risk involved in these experiments, it seems best to give it a separate name. For lack of a better term let us call it *developmental risk*. By that term will be meant the uncertainty as to the return to be realized from the investment of capital in the production of a new commodity or of a new capital good, due to the possibility that it may not find the expected market, or may not perform the work for which it was intended.

To return now to the general distinction between static and dynamic losses, we find that there are several important differences between them. A static loss results either from the physical destruction of the object, in which case the entire loss is a net loss to society, or from the change of possession, as the result of carelessness or fraud, which may or may not in itself involve a social loss, according to the efficiency with which the object is utilized by the old and the new possessor. A dynamic loss results from a decrease in the value of the object, and in a progressive society the very conditions which cause the loss to the individual generally make it certain that society will be benefited by the change.

In the second place static losses usually affect one unit or several units of the same or of different kinds of capital goods, while dynamic losses affect all the units of a given class at the same time. Fire may destroy one building here and another there, while the great majority of similar buildings go unscathed; but an invention which takes the value out of one machine takes it out of all similar machines at the same time, and a change in consumption which causes a falling off in the demand for any kind of commodity affects the value of all existing stocks of that commodity in the hands of manufacturers and dealers.

In the third place static losses occur with more or less approach to regularity, if comparisons are made over considerable periods of time, while dynamic losses are very irregular in the time and place of their appearance. Statistics show that the losses by fire in different decades bear an approximately fixed ratio to the possibility of loss. But dynamic losses in one period may vary greatly from those in another, and in any particular industry the amount to be expected in a given time is almost wholly indeterminable. In other words, if large groups of similar cases are considered, the uncertainty as to the amount of the loss to be anticipated from the action of static forces is far less than the uncertainty about the amount of the dynamic loss. Or, as risk and uncertainty are correlative, we may say that the risk of dynamic loss is greater than the risk of static loss.

These points of unlikeness between static and dynamic losses are of great importance for the technique of insurance. Because dynamic losses are so irregular and incalculable in their appearance, it is impossible to estimate with any approach to certainty what funds must be accumulated to meet them; and because when they occur they affect entire classes of goods at the same time, it is impossible to compensate those who suffer loss, at the expense of others who are exposed to the same danger, but are so fortunate as to escape. The result is that while dynamic losses are the ones which most deserve compensation, because in general they occur through no negligence or fault on the part of the persons suffering them, and while they are the ones which society can best afford to make good, since they are usually accompanied by a net social gain, they are also the ones against which the least protection is furnished by existing methods of insurance.

The distinction between static and dynamic losses is as important for the theory of risk as it is for the technique of insurance, but to attempt at this place to show what economic consequences flow from it, would be to anticipate a considerable part of the argument that is to follow. Its significance will appear most prominently in the discussion of the activity of the capitalist-entrepreneur and its relation to risk.

Somewhat analogous to the distinction here drawn between static and dynamic losses is that made by Mangoldt between technical and economic losses.[5] A technical loss is due to the failure of an investment of capital to yield the physical product expected of it. He cites as illustrations an unexpectedly small increase from an investment in agriculture, the failure of a machine to perform the work expected of it, and the loss of a ship at sea. An economic loss is due to an unfavorable discrepancy between the anticipated value of the product and the value actually realized. As an illustration he cites the case of a railroad, physically, or "technically," able to perform the work expected of it, but yielding less than the usual reward to the capital invested, because the demand for its services is not so great as was anticipated.[6]

Now it is evident that Mangoldt's economic losses are all dynamic. They are connected with improvements in methods of production or with changes in human wants. But not all of his technical losses are static. The failure of a machine to do the work expected of it may be of either kind. It is static if the machine is of a form already in use, and its failure to work is due to a flaw in its construction, or to the accidental destruction of the machine itself; it is dynamic, however, if the machine is of a new and untried type, and its failure is caused by a mistake of judgment as to the way in which it will perform its work. That Mangoldt includes in the technical group this kind of dynamic loss, which I have called developmental, is shown by his statement that "the danger of failure (in the case of technical risks) is naturally greatest where there is something essentially new about the commodity, means of production, or method."[7]

Mangoldt's purpose in making this classification was to identify the kinds of risks which according to his theory of distribution

---

5 H. von Mangoldt: *Volkswirthschaftslehre,* Stuttgart, 1868, p. 184.

6 There is a striking similarity between Mangoldt's classification and that developed at greater length by Professor E. A. Ross. (See "Uncertainty as a Factor in Production," *Annals of the American Academy,* vol. VIII, p. 92.) Professor Ross dwells upon the importance of the distinction between uncertainty as to the relation of outlay to product, and uncertainty as to the relation of product to price; but it is with their influence upon production that he is primarily concerned, and only incidentally does he touch upon their relation to distribution.

7 *Ibid.,* 186. "Am grössten ist natürlich die Gefahr des Misslingens da, wo es sich um etwas wesentlich Neues in Bezug auf Gegenstand, Productionsmittel oder Methode handelt."

it is the special function of the entrepreneur to bear. In an isolated economy, he says, economic loss could occur only as a result
of technical loss. When production for exchange begins, there
arises the possibility of economic loss not occasioned by an attendant technical loss, and then the entrepreneur appears. He
produces goods for exchange, and consequently is exposed to the
danger of economic loss. It is for bearing this risk that he obtains
his special reward. I must postpone for the present a complete
discussion of Mangoldt's theory. To indicate its imperfection it
is sufficient to point out two things. In the first place it is not true
that a man living in isolation could suffer an economic loss only
as result of a technical loss. A Robinson Crusoe might accumulate
a stock of some commodity with the expectation that it would be
of great service to him, and afterwards discover a substitute so
much more efficient that he would no longer attach any value to
his former accumulation. In the second place no important
service to economic theory can be rendered by a classification of
functions which rests on a distinction of so little significance as
the one that separates these two classes of risks.

Of other classifications of risk which have been attempted I
will mention but one, and that only because of a question of
distribution with which its author has connected it. Professor
H. C. Emery distinguishes risks of production from speculative
risks.[8] Risks of production are enumerated by him without being
defined; but speculative risks, we are told, are "the risks of price
fluctuations affecting the whole market, that is, the distinctively
Conjunctur-risks." It is evident that for the most part this classification, like Mangoldt's and Ross's, is based on the distinction
between uncertainty as to physical product and uncertainty as to
value; and as the risk undertaken by an entrepreneur who puts
new goods on the market is not considered, the risks included in
the two groups fall for the most part under the head of static
and dynamic risks respectively. Of the risks of production, we are
told, some "are borne by the laborer, some by the capitalist, most
of them by the entrepreneur," while the assumption of speculative risks is the function of the speculator, whose economic

8 Henry Crosby Emery: "The Place of the Speculator in the Theory of Distribution," *Publications of the American Economic Association*, vol. i, no. i,
p. 104.

identity it is the purpose of the article to help determine. As I shall have occasion to consider some of Professor Emery's arguments when I speak of the relation of the speculator to insurance, I have thought it best to mention the principle on which his classification of risks is based.

Let us briefly review the conclusions that we have reached as a result of the foregoing analysis. The only risks that are important for our purposes are those that are incurred as a result of participation in economic life. The element of personal suffering involved in many losses is a disturbing factor which we are obliged to leave out of account. Partly because this is usually present in the risks to which labor is exposed, and partly on account of the limited extent to which these risks can be transferred to other persons, we shall confine our attention to the effect of risk on capital and its employment.

For theoretical purposes the most significant classification of economic risks to capital is the division into static and dynamic risks. Static risks are those which are inseparable from any form of economic activity, and which will therefore be present in a stationary society as much as in one that is either progressive or retrogressive. They are involved in the possibility of loss as a result of the action of the forces of nature or of the carelessness or criminality of human beings. Dynamic risks are connected with the possibility of loss resulting from dynamic changes. As the degree of risk is correlative with uncertainty, the greatest amount of risk is associated with those kinds of dynamic change that occur with the greatest irregularity. Changes in population and wealth occur with comparative uniformity, and therefore involve little unexpected loss. Changes in human wants are less uniform and produce a greater degree of uncertainty. Changes in machinery and in methods of production are still more irregular in their appearance, and it is with them that the greatest amount of uncertainty is connected. A special form of dynamic risk, and one of great importance in modern life, is the developmental risk incurred by those who make investments of capital in the production of new and untried commodities, whether they are intended for consumption or for producing consumption goods.

I need not stop to repeat what has been said about the differences between static and dynamic risks, or about the importance of the other classifications which we discussed. I will close this lengthy chapter with a word of explanation as to the bearing which any such classification has upon the general theory of risk. So far as the effect of the risk itself on economic activity is concerned, its place in any classification has practically no significance. Risk is the objective correlative of uncertainty about the relation between present outlay and future return. Upon a person considering the advisability of any investment of capital, the influence of a given degree of uncertainty about the outcome will in general be the same, whatever may be the location of the uncertainty or the source of the possible loss. The only question which concerns him is as to the degree of risk involved. It is in the discussion of special phases of the theory of risk, and still more in the examination of the different devices which society has adopted for counteracting its unfavorable influence, that the importance of the classifications given above will appear.

THE COST OF RISK

Risk and uncertainty are the objective and subjective aspects of apparent variability in the course of natural events. Whatever effect risk may have on economic activity is brought about through the psychological influence of uncertainty. The fundamental facts of human nature on which the doctrine of risk is based are that in economic affairs uncertainty is in general a disagreeable state of mind, and that the disagreeableness increases as the uncertainty increases. This means more than that every man prefers a certain gain to a probable one of the same amount, a sure return of five per cent to a possible return of five per cent which may never be realized. It means that he prefers a certain return of five per cent to an uncertain return which may be nothing or may be ten per cent, with no indication of where it will fall between the two limits. As a general rule uncertainty exercises a repellent influence in economic life.

This general statement, however, is subject to numerous qualifications. In the first place it is evident that the same degree of risk does not have the same amount of influence on all men. This may be because different men form different estimates of the degree of risk involved in any undertaking. In such a case the influence which will be exerted will depend upon the subjective estimate of the objective risk; for it is only through the subjective uncertainty that the objective fact makes its influence felt. It may be because of differences in the mental and moral nature of the men. A venturesome, self-reliant man may find little unpleasantness, or possibly even a positive pleasure, in assuming a risk from which a timid man would shrink; and on the other hand one with little prudence and foresight will readily incur a risk which a more rational man would avoid. To some the excitement involved in assuming risks becomes so attractive that it is in itself a sufficient inducement to lead them to expose themselves to

24

almost certain loss. The gambling instinct has entirely overcome what may be called in contrast the business instinct. The difference may be due to unlike personal relationships. A man with others dependent upon him for support will be less ready to take chances than one who has only himself to consider. Finally, it may be due to inequalities in the amount of wealth possessed by the men in question. Other things being equal, the man with a large fortune will be less unwilling to expose a definite sum to a given risk than one with little wealth.

In the second place, the same person is not always affected in the same way by risks which he estimates alike. This variation may be brought about in several ways. It may be because of non-economic considerations. If the odor of respectability attaches to an uncertain form of investment, while a safer form has plebeian associations, these facts may more than counterbalance the effect of the larger risk. It may be on account of differences in the nature of the risks themselves. Adam Smith was the first to point out the unlike effects produced by a great chance of winning a small amount, and a small chance of winning a large amount. Readiness to assume the latter kind of risk is frequently far greater than would be justified by its true actuarial value. It is to this peculiarity of human nature that the excess in the amount of capital invested in certain extra-hazardous occupations, such as gold-mining, is partly to be attributed. Finally, with changes in a man's economic condition, his reluctance to incur risk also changes. As his wealth increases the marginal utility of a fixed sum becomes smaller, and for that reason his unwillingness to expose it to a definite risk also diminishes.

How far the economic behavior of mankind in the face of uncertainty is affected by such considerations as these, could be determined only by an inductive study. In the discussion of the general theory of risk we are obliged to neglect all these disturbing elements, and to assume for man's conduct a degree of regularity which does not actually prevail. Except when a definite statement to the contrary is made, the argument proceeds on the assumption that the effect of a given degree of uncertainty is the same upon all men, regardless of any peculiarities in the nature of the risk or of the persons assuming it.

The first proposition to be established is that uncertainty in economic affairs is an evil, causing a net loss to society in addition to all the losses occasioned by the occurrence of unfavorable events. A certain amount of capital will be accidentally destroyed during the coming year. On account of the uncertainty as to the amount of loss which will occur, the economic condition at the end of the year will be less favorable than it would be if the same loss were to occur, but the time and place of its occurrence could be accurately foreseen. Or, to state the same thing in a different way, if none of the possible accidental loss should actually occur, but the present degree of uncertainty should continue, the condition at the end of the year would be less favorable than it would have been if the uncertainty had been absent as well as the loss.

This net loss, due to the existence of risk, is the result of the repellent influence of uncertainty upon normal human beings. Uncertainty is a form of disutility which no one will voluntarily incur unless something is to be gained by so doing. The first place where its influence can be detected is in the accumulation of capital. If risk were uniform in all kinds of investment, the rate of accumulation in a dynamic society would evidently depend partly on the degree of risk to which capital was exposed; and with unequal degrees of risk in different investments the same relation exists, though it is more difficult to trace.

But this is properly a dynamic question, to which we shall return later on. In a static society the effect of uncertainty is visible only in the employment of the capital already in existence. In an ideal static state capital would be so apportioned that every unit of it would be equally productive. The same thing would be true of an approximate static state on the assumption that there was the same degree of risk involved in all forms of investment. But the real world shows no such uniformity of risk. The static state which would evolve, if dynamic changes were to cease, would be one in which different forms of investment would involve unequal degrees of uncertainty. This condition of things would prevent the perfect static apportionment of capital. No one would be willing to make investments in hazardous enterprises with the expectation of receiving only the same average net return that he could obtain in safe investments. The apportionment of capital would be so made that the net return in different investments would vary directly as the degree of uncertainty involved in them. The flow of capital into hazardous enterprises would cease while its marginal productivity in them was still enough above its marginal productivity in safe investments to yield the additional net reward necessary to induce investors to incur the risk. If the degree of risk in some form of investment is such that it requires a net return of two per cent above the rate in safe investments to induce any capitalist to assume it, there is no way in which competition can do away with the extra two per cent so long as the degree of risk remains unchanged. The flow of capital into the industry ceases while the return to it is still two per cent above the return in safe investments. The extra two per cent is the incentive necessary to induce any investor to incur the risk, and for that reason no one will bring down the rate towards the normal level by offering capital for a smaller reward.

So far in our discussion we have made no allowance for the important consequences of the influence of the law of diminishing utility on the reluctance to incur risk. Every unit added to a man's wealth has less value to him than the preceding unit. If a man with $10,000 ventures it in an enterprise in which he runs a risk of losing it all or winning another $10,000, the $10,000 he will win in case of success will have far less utility to him than the $10,000 he will lose in case of failure. And if he ventures only $1,000, it is still true, in a less degree, that the additional $1,000 will have less utility to him than the marginal $1,000 he already possesses. A perfectly fair wager, therefore, in which due allowance is made for the different degrees of utility of the sum wagered to the two parties, is never economically justifiable. Thus if two men, to whom $1,000 has the same marginal utility, wager it on the toss of a penny, the one who loses will necessarily lose more than is gained by the one who wins. There is a net loss to the two by the transaction.

The effect of this psychological principle is obvious. The amount of the extra remuneration which will be required to induce the investor to incur a risk is influenced by the diminishing utility to him of additional units of capital. If he possesses 5 units of capital, we may let 10 represent the utility of the first unit, 9 of the second, 8 of the third, 7 of the fourth, and 6 of the fifth.[1] Then the total utility of his capital is represented by 40. If the utility of additional units continued to diminish at the same rate, 5 more would have the utility respectively of 5, 4, 3, 2 and 1, or a total of 15. Therefore, he would subject himself to the chance of losing all his capital or of winning another equal amount, for this reason alone, only when in his judgment the chance of success was to the chance of failure as 40 to 15; and he would incur the risk of losing his marginal unit or of gaining another unit, only when the chances were as 6 to 5. Or if we assume equal chances of success or failure, the sum to be gained would have to exceed the sum to be lost by a sufficient amount to make the utility of the two sums equal.

It is evident, then, that the effect of man's natural unwillingness to subject himself to uncertainty in his economic activity, reinforced by the effect of the diminishing utility of successive increments of wealth, will be such an apportionment of the existing amount of capital among different industries that the return to it will vary with the degree of uncertainty. The most productive apportionment of capital would evidently be the one in which the marginal productivity was the same in all industries. The loss which society would suffer in a static state on account of the existence of risk would be due to the diminution in the productivity of capital caused by its uneconomic apportionment. If for the sake of simplicity we assume that all the forms of investment of capital are capable of being arranged in two groups, such that the risk in the first is twice as great as that in the second, capital will be so apportioned that its productivity in the former will exceed its productivity in the latter. Compared with the productivity under the uniform apportionment that would prevail if the risk were equalized, the former group will show a net increase, and the latter a net decrease. The cost of the risk cannot be ascertained by subtracting the wealth created by the capital in the less productive group from the wealth which would be created by the same capital if it were as productive as that in the other group. The diminished productivity of that part

1 Adapted from J. B. Clark: "Insurance and Business Profit," *Quarterly Journal of Economics*, vol. vii, p. 44.

of the capital is partially offset by the increased productivity of the other part. The cost of the risk is the difference between the net excess of the product created in the more hazardous group, as compared with the amount that would be created by the same capital in a static apportionment, and the net deficiency in the product of the other group.

This net loss due to the existence of uncertainty must not be confounded with the loss of capital which results from the actual occurrence of the uncertain event. The former is always of the kind that I have called negative. The existing amount of capital and labor would create a certain amount of wealth if it were apportioned in the most productive way. It creates a smaller amount when the realization of this apportionment is prevented by the existence of risk. The difference between these two sums, that is, the wealth whose creation is made impossible by the uneconomic apportionment, is the cost of risk to a static society. A full discussion of the connection between the chance losses and gains due to the occurrence or non-occurrence of uncertain events, and the negative loss caused by the existence of the uncertainty itself, can be better undertaken in the next chapter, when we come to consider them from the point of view of the person who assumes the risk.

It must be noticed also that the statement that risk or uncertainty entails a burden upon society by no means implies that society would necessarily be better off if all risk were avoided. If the uncertainty involved in existing forms of investment could be abolished, with no additional expense for protection from accidental loss, and no change in the amount that actually occurred, the result would be a saving to society of the net loss which the risk now causes. But if the uncertainty were avoided by withdrawing capital from all investments in which more than the minimum degree of risk is involved, society would suffer a great diminution of well-being. The fact that capital can obtain the extra reward necessary to induce it to enter a hazardous employment shows that society values so highly the product of the industry that it prefers to bear the extra expense rather than content itself with the products of safe investments.

We will conclude our discussion of the cost of risk to society with a consideration of the distribution of the burden among the different categories of economic persons. The laborer as such is not affected by inequalities in the degree of risk to which different units of capital are exposed. The amount of capital in a hazardous investment is limited, and its productivity is for that reason abnormally high; but there is nothing in that fact to interfere with the static apportionment of labor, which will make its productivity and its reward everywhere the same. The immediate return to the laborer will be the same in an industry in which the capital is exposed to a high degree of risk as it is in one involving little risk.

Obviously this is not true of capital. The principle that we are trying to establish is that the return to capital from investments with unequal degrees of risk will vary as the uncertainty varies. The additional reward, however, is not, strictly speaking, an abnormal gain, like that which might be obtained by a capitalist who controlled the supply of a valuable natural product. Other capital is not prevented by an external force from coming in and obtaining a share in the extra reward. It cannot properly be said, therefore, that some capital gains at the expense of the rest on account of inequalities in the risk to which it is exposed. The capital in the hazardous investment is performing a greater social service, and for that reason obtains a greater reward.

It is upon the consumer that the whole burden of risk in a static society would fall. The extra reward of capital can be obtained only through the medium of higher prices. The commodities produced by the hazardous industries cannot be sold as cheap as they would be if the uncertainty were removed. Whoever consumes any such commodity bears a part of the burden of risk. The extra price paid by all the persons who use commodities whose production involves so much risk that the capital engaged in producing them obtains a reward higher than it could obtain under the ideal static adjustment, is from this point of view the cost of risk to society. But here again allowance must be made for the gain which partially offsets the loss. If the prices of commodities produced in hazardous industries are higher than the static level, the prices of other commodities, produced in industries free from risk, must be below that level. The net loss to consumers would be ascertained by subtracting from the excess in price of the former class of commodities the saving made by those who purchased the latter class.[2]

This brings us to the final point to be noticed in this connection. The burden of risk is not borne equally by all consumers, nor is it distributed according to the amounts spent in the purchase of consumption goods. A far larger share of it is borne by one whose purchases are confined to the products of hazardous industries than by one who buys almost exclusively articles in whose creation little risk is involved. A consumer might even realize a net gain on account of risk, if it were possible for him to confine his purchases to consumption goods whose price is below the static level. The burden of risk is borne by those who consume the products of the hazardous industries, and it is distributed according to the amounts spent in the purchase of such commodities, with proper allowance for the savings realized from the purchase of the abnormally low priced goods.

The following are the principal points that we have sought to establish in the present chapter: Risk affects economic activity through the psychological influence of uncertainty. Uncertainty is a kind of disutility, and it will not be borne without some inducement. Its influence is largely enhanced by the fact that the utility of successive increments of capital gradually diminishes. In a dynamic society the effect of uncertainty is seen in a retardation of the rate of accumulating capital. In a static society the inequality in the amount of uncertainty involved in different investments causes such an apportionment of capital among them that its productivity varies as the degree of risk to which it is exposed. The most advantageous apportionment would be the ideal static condition, in which all units were equally productive. The loss of productivity caused by the uneconomic employment of existing capital is the cost of risk in a static state. This burden is borne by consumers, and it is distributed among them according to the relative amounts spent for consumption goods whose creation involves comparatively high degrees of risk, and for those produced with little or no risk.

2 If the commodity produced in the hazardous industry is a capital good instead of a consumption good, the extra cost is first borne by the purchasers of the capital good. It hardly seems necessary to point out how it is shifted from person to person until it finally rests upon the one who uses the consumption good which the capital good helps to create.

CHAPTER IV

THE ASSUMPTION OF RISK

The existence of risk in an approximate static state causes an economic loss. The assumption of risk, on the other hand, is a source of gain to society, and a part of the gain is obtained by the risk-takers as their special reward. We will first consider in what sense and under what conditions risk-taking is socially productive, and then examine the nature and amount of the net reward received by the person who assumes the risk.

It is evident that risk-taking is not productive in the same sense in which capital and labor are. It has no claim to rank as a third coördinate productive agent. All wealth is created by labor and capital, and by them alone. No one would think of attempting to divide the social product into three parts, saying that one was created by capital, another by labor, and the third by risk-taking. The very incongruity of these statements is sufficient to indicate that the term productivity, when applied to risk-taking, is used in a somewhat loose and inaccurate way. The fact is that, as we have already shown, inequalities in the degree of risk involved in different investments of capital bring about inequalities in productivity. Capital in a hazardous investment will create more product than that which is not exposed to risk. It is evidently not the risk-taking that creates the extra product, but the capital itself.

It would hardly seem worth while to insist on a point which is so nearly self-evident if there were not instances of confusion of thought resulting from the failure to make this distinction. The difficulty may be due to an unconscious attempt to think in terms of productivity and sacrifice at the same time. Risk-taking is rewarded in the same sense as abstinence, or labor, considered as a form of sacrifice; but the reward which it receives is no more created by the risk-taking than interest by abstinence, or wages by the unpleasant feelings aroused by labor. The extra reward is created by the capital that receives it. Risk-taking is productive only in the secondary sense that it occasions the increase in the productivity of capital.

Even in this sense it is manifest that the assumption of risk is not always productive, but only when it takes place under certain conditions. That it is not productive when the risk is voluntarily and unnecessarily created, as in the case of a wager, is self-evident; for the gain to society from the assumption of a risk can never be as great as the loss due to its existence. It is only when the risk is a necessary and unavoidable incident of socially desirable economic activity that its assumption can be advantageous to society. Moreover, there is need of a still further limitation. The assumption of an economic risk is not *per se* a good thing for society. It is desirable only when the commodity whose creation involves the risk is one for which the demand is so intense that it can command a price high enough to replace all capital lost in its production, and leave a net return at least as large as the usual rate of interest.

Under these conditions it would be advantageous to society to have capital assume all risks in which the probability of gain exceeds the probability of loss. The assumption of an infinite number of such chances would result in a net gain. But we have already seen that the influence of the unwillingness of men to incur risk, and of the diminishing utility of additional increments of wealth, causes the assumption of risks by individuals to stop far short of the point of equal chances. A risk will be assumed only when the commodity created as a consequence is so important that consumers are willing to make good all losses to the capital as a whole and to give to each capitalist a special reward for incurring the risk.

A clear conception of the nature of the service that the assumption of risk within these limits performs, may be obtained by considering the loss entailed by a contraction of risk-taking. We will assume that society has reached an approximately static condition, in which the highest degree of risk involved in any form of investment of capital may be represented by 10, and the extra reward necessary to induce capitalists to incur it, by 5. Now let us imagine a slight increase in the reluctance to assume risk, so that it would require an extra reward 6 to attract capital into the most hazardous investment, which was before assumed for the reward 5; and that the demand for the product of that industry is so inelastic that none of it will be consumed at the price necessary to yield the larger reward. That commodity would no longer be produced. The most hazardous investment now undertaken would involve a degree of uncertainty which we will represent by 8, and the necessary extra reward under the new conditions we will assume to be 4. How would society be affected by the change?

In the first place, consumers would have lost the entire product of the abandoned industries, commodities which they wanted with sufficient intensity to make them willing to pay the price necessary to yield the extra reward 5 to the capital producing them. On the other hand, the capital and labor withdrawn from the non-hazardous enterprises would have to find employment in fields already occupied. Whatever industry any of it entered would yield a larger amount of physical product than before. But the price of each commodity was already so adjusted as to furnish a market for just the amount produced and no more. To find purchasers for the new product it would be necessary to lower the price. The amount of the necessary reduction would vary in different industries according to the elasticity of the demand for the different products. In course of time a new adjustment of the productive forces would be reached, in which again the supply of the product of each industry would just suffice to meet the demand for it. But the new supplies of commodities of different kinds must be catering to wants of a lower degree of intensity than those formerly satisfied by the articles produced in the hazardous enterprises. This is proved by the fact that society was willing to give the extra reward to the capitalists who would create the latter. If the productivity of capital and labor is measured in terms of social well-being, every unit of capital and every unit of labor is now less productive than it was before. The result is a slight falling off in the incentive to productive effort. In the end there would probably be some increase in the consumption of the products of the safe investments, some diminution in the amount of capital, and some reduction in the length of the labor day. If all these things, however, were to be considered as gains, they would not be enough to offset the loss that society would suffer through its inability to obtain the products of the hazardous industry. The social service rendered by the assumption of a risk for which society is willing to pay is the satisfaction of wants of a higher degree of intensity than would otherwise be reached. The result is an increase in the productivity of all capital and labor—that is, in their power to minister to human well-being.

So far we have been considering the productivity of risk-taking from the point of view of society. We will now consider it from the side of the risk-taker. In a static state, where production and consumption are properly correlated, every producer who carries a risk above the minimum will receive a special reward for its assumption. Competition cannot take it away from him, because no one is willing to bear the risk unless he is rewarded for doing so. It is obtained through the obstruction which the risk offers to the free flow of capital into the investment. There is less of the product of the hazardous industry created than there would be if the risk were absent. As a result the price is higher than it would be under a perfect static adjustment. Out of this abnormally high price comes the extra reward for the risk-taker.

This brings out at once the method by which the amount of this extra reward is determined. On the supposition that all the units of a commodity are produced under conditions involving the same degree of risk, and that this risk has the same influence on all investors, it is clear that the reward which may be obtained for assuming it is definitely fixed. If, for example, the risk involved is represented by 5, and the reward necessary to induce capital to incur it by 2, no one can permanently obtain a higher reward for assuming it. Capital will continue to come into the industries involving the risk, until the increase of product has lowered the price to a point where it yields the extra reward 2 and no more; and, on the other hand, the reward cannot be brought below that point, because by hypothesis no investor is willing to incur the risk for any less. The amount of the reward to be obtained by assuming any degree of risk is determined by the disutility involved in enduring the resulting uncertainty.

But it is not the fact that all units of every product are created under conditions involving the same degree of risk. The demand for some commodity may be so great that a part of the supply has to be produced under exceptionally dangerous circumstances. The capital engaged in producing this part of it must be rewarded in proportion to the risk to which it is exposed. If all other expenses of production are everywhere equal, the necessity of paying extra for the extra risk will make this part of the supply the most expensive. The price of all units of the commodity, therefore, will be fixed at the point that will cover the expense of producing this portion of it. The capital that is exposed to a lower degree of risk in creating the same commodity will receive a larger reward than the sacrifice of its possessor calls for. This extra gain is of the kind which is commonly spoken of as rent. It naturally attaches itself to that portion of the capital which is invested in land.

Nor is it true that a given degree of risk has the same influence on all investors. For various reasons, of which we have already spoken, some men are less reluctant to incur risks than others. The reward which they will demand will be correspondingly less. Let us divide all investors into three classes, of different degrees of unwillingness to incur risk, so that for assuming the risk 5 they will respectively require the extra rewards 3, 2 and 1. If the demand for the commodities in whose production the risk 5 is involved is so great that it is necessary to use some of the capital of the most reluctant investors in producing them, it is evident that the price of the commodity will be fixed at the point that will give these investors the extra reward they demand. As the price of all units of the commodity must be the same, all capital will receive the same extra reward 3. Those investors who would be willing to incur the risk for 2 or 1 will receive a larger reward than is made necessary by their individual sacrifice. This extra gain might be called a risk-taker's surplus. It is one form of the producer's surplus, of which Professor Marshall speaks.[1]

Making allowance for these inequalities in the degree of risk

[1] It hardly needs to be mentioned that we can speak of such a surplus only when comparison is made with the sacrifice of the individual investor. According to the productivity theory capital is rewarded in proportion to the product it creates, and not in proportion to the sacrifice of its owner. Capital that is equally productive receives the same reward. The impossibility of correlating individual rewards with individual sacrifices is the rock on which any sacrifice theory of distribution goes to pieces. The recognition of the existence of the so-called producer's surplus is a virtual abandonment of the whole position.

and in reluctance to incur risk, we shall have to modify our statement of the law which regulates the amount of the reward for risk-taking. That reward will be fixed at the point which will make the most reluctant investor whose capital is needed willing to incur the highest degree of risk involved in the creation of any part of the product for which consumers are willing to pay. There is a margin of risk-taking, just as there is a margin of labor or of abstinence; and in the case of any given degree of risk, it is the marginal risk-taker whose reluctance fixes the amount of reward which is obtained for assuming it.

It may be well to bring out more clearly than we have yet done the exact nature of the net reward for risk-taking. It is not always easy to distinguish between the effect of the assumption of risk and the effect of accidental gains and losses. The statement that the assumption of risk yields a special reward is not intended to imply that every risk-taker will be better off at the end of a year, or even at the end of a number of years, than he was when he put his capital into the hazardous investment. I do not refer now to the loss he may suffer on account of having underestimated the chances of failure or the possibility of disaster. Even though all risks could be and were accurately estimated, it is evident that all persons who assumed them could not fare alike. Some of the possible loss would be realized and some would not. One person might suffer early and seriously, while another might escape for a number of years. Uncertainty as to the amount of loss which each investor will actually suffer is an essential element of the risk. Without the possibility of varying results for different investors there would be no question of risk to consider. If the different men formed the same estimate of the risk they were assuming, they would naturally make the same preparations to meet the accidental loss. The one who was early overtaken by it might reach the end of a period of years far worse off than he would have been if he had confined himself to safe investments. The one who went through unscathed would, on the other hand, be far better off. The important point to notice is that the reward for risk-taking is obtained by both the fortunate and the unfortunate investor, although its amount cannot be determined directly from the results of the two investments. The man who has suffered the loss whose possible occurrence was foreseen is better off than he would have been if his capital had not been abnormally productive; and the man who anticipated the possible occurrence of a loss which he did not suffer is also better off on account of the abnormal productivity of his capital. The reward for risk-taking could be identified only in the case of an investor who suffered just such an amount of loss as past experience had shown might on the average be expected. The return which such an investor would realize from the use of his capital would exceed pure interest, or the return in safe investments, by a certain amount, which would be the net reward for assuming the risk. As it is the degree of uncertainty which determines the unwillingness of investors to enter the industry, this net reward would vary according to the previous uncertainty as to the probable variation of the actual loss from the average.[2]

Additional light may be shed upon this point by a consideration of the way in which the extra reward for assuming risk is obtained. Let us consider the conduct of a person who is planning to use his capital in a more or less hazardous employment. He has to look forward to two kinds of losses. In the first place he will have to meet certain definite expenses involved in replacing various capital goods as they are used up in the process of production. For this purpose he will accumulate what is called an amortization fund. In the second place he will expect to suffer some loss through the occurrence of the events whose possibility constitutes the risk of the investment. His accumulation for this purpose is commonly spoken of as his insurance fund. In considering the advisability of making the investment, he will allow for both these forms of loss, and his decision will depend upon

---

[2] Marshall recognizes the existence of this net premium for risk-taking: "As a rule, a person will not enter on a risky business unless, other things being equal, he expects to gain from it more than he would in other trades open to him, after his probable losses had been deducted from his probable gains on a fair actuarial estimate." (Alfred Marshall, *Principles of Economics*, 3d ed., p. 693.)

Pantaleoni, on the contrary, apparently overlooks it: "Mere compensation, however, for the risk of an undertaking cannot constitute a *normal source of rent;* for if this compensation has been estimated strictly in proportion to the risk, it must, on an average for a number of years, be exactly equivalent to the latter, so that the net rent left would be equal to zero; whilst, on the other hand, if the compensation is not commensurate with the risk, it is anti-hedonic in its origin, the disproportion being due to ignorance as to the frequency and magnitude of the risk." (Maffeo Pantaleoni, *Pure Economics,* translated by T. B. Bruce. London, 1898, p. 279.)

the amount of the net return which he may hope to realize. He will embark in the industry only on the condition that the price of the product is high enough to enable him to accumulate these two funds and to obtain in addition the usual reward for the use of his capital.

Now it is clear that the amounts of the two funds cannot be determined in exactly the same way. To meet definitely foreseen losses he can obtain no more than just enough to cover them. If he were seeking a larger return, other capital would come in, and the price of the product would fall. The size of the insurance fund, however, cannot be determined by the amount of the actual loss, since it is about the amount of loss that will be suffered that the uncertainty exists. If the attempt were made to secure enough to cover all possible loss, it is clear that other capital would come in and accept a somewhat smaller return, on the chance that the possible loss might not be realized. But it is equally clear that the influx of new capital will cease before the price of the product has been brought so low that the insurance fund is reduced to the amount of the average loss. The amount of the net reward for risk-taking will be determined by the relation between the size of the insurance fund which can be accumulated, after the competition of different investors has reduced it to a minimum, and the amount of accidental loss which is expected to occur. According to the principles which we have sought to establish, the influx of new capital will cease while the price of the product enables investors to accumulate such a fund in excess of the probable amount of accidental loss; and the amount of this extra accumulation will be the greater, the more the uncertainty as to the variation of the actual loss from the average. If we assume that in a series of years the losses which an investor suffers just equal the amount which previous experience had shown to be the average, he will be left at the end of the period with a net gain, which is his reward for assuming risk.

One other point remains to be noticed. In speaking of the difference between the amortization fund and the insurance fund, the assumption was made for the purpose of convenience that it was possible to distinguish between the certain and the uncertain loss by some external characteristic, such as the source of the loss or the form in which it occurs. The real distinction. however, lies in the element of uncertainty itself, and nowhere else. Preparation for any kind of certain loss is made by means of the amortization fund; preparation for any kind of uncertain loss by the insurance fund. Let us illustrate this point with an example.

In certain industries capital has to lie idle during part of the year. The idleness in itself causes a loss. To make up for it, the capital will have to be abnormally productive during the months in which it is active. If the period of idleness is the same every year, so that its duration and the consequent loss can be definitely foreseen, the amount of the accumulation to meet the loss will also be fixed; and, in the absence of other disturbing forces, it will be fixed at the amount of the foreseen loss. If, however, there is uncertainty about the duration of the idleness, there will be the same uncertainty about the amount of accumulation which will be necessary to cover the loss; and in determining its size, allowance will be made for the possibility that the actual loss may exceed the average. In the former case we have an amortization fund, and in the latter an insurance fund. Finally, if a certain minimum of loss can be foreseen, and the only uncertainty concerns the extent to which the actual loss may exceed the minimum, the accumulation to meet the certain part of it will be of the former kind, and that to meet the uncertain part, of the latter.

The definiteness which the application of this principle gives to the significance of the term insurance is evidently not in accord with the ordinary commercial usage of the word. I shall refer to that point again when I come to speak more at length of insurance as an economic institution. Moreover, it is not claimed that investors in all cases actually go through the calculations involved in the two ways of making accumulations. There is usually no literal separation of the amortization fund from the insurance fund. It is the general result of an investment by which the conduct of men is influenced. Even in those cases in which a definite sum is set aside to meet some special form of accidental loss, while this accumulation is usually spoken of as an insurance fund, it is not customary to make any distinction between the part which is to replace the minimum of loss that is certain to occur, and that for the additional possible loss, whose occurrence is uncertain. The so-called insurance fund is very apt to include the accumulation to meet all the loss of a certain kind, whether or not its occurrence can be definitely foreseen. Still the fact remains that the competition of investors with one another will force down the amount of the possible accumulations to the point where it will equal the amount of the certain loss of all kinds, plus the average amount of the uncertain loss, plus an additional increment, the size of which will depend on the degree of uncertainty as to the actual amount of the uncertain loss, and will be in no way affected by the amount of the certain loss.

The conclusions that we have reached in the present chapter may be briefly summarized as follows: Risk-taking is productive only in a secondary sense; it increases the productivity of capital. The person who assumes a risk under the right economic conditions receives a special reward. The amount of the reward depends on the degree of risk and on the unwillingness of men to incur it. The reward is obtained through the accumulation of a fund to meet future losses. For those losses whose occurrence can be foreseen an amortization fund is accumulated. Its size is fixed by competition at the amount of the foreseen loss. For those losses whose occurrence is uncertain an insurance fund is accumulated. Its size exceeds the probable amount of loss as determined from past experience. The excess varies with the degree of uncertainty about the amount of loss that will be suffered. This extra accumulation is the reward for risk-taking.

CHAPTER V

THE REWARD FOR RISK-TAKING

In our discussion hitherto we have as far as possible avoided the use of language which involved a prejudgment as to the economic character of the reward for risk-taking. It is now time to turn our attention to the consideration of this phase of the question. We shall seek to determine under which of the categories of distribution the reward for assuming risk falls. Incidentally we shall have to notice one or two of the attempts that have been made to identify this peculiar reward with the income of the entrepreneur. In conclusion, we shall consider the advisability of adopting the suggestion that the reward for risk-taking be made an independent category of distribution, coördinate with wages, interest and profit.

It seems to be a self-evident proposition that no one can assume a risk in economic affairs unless he has something to lose. As it is capital that is exposed to danger, it would seem that it must be the owner of the capital, that is, the capitalist, who assumes the possibility of loss. A society in which one class of people owned the capital, and another class enjoyed the unrestricted privilege of exposing it to risk, would soon suffer economic shipwreck. It is the possessor of capital who is interested in its safety, and he seeks to protect it by demanding for its use a return commensurate with the chance of loss to which it is exposed. In just what sense a man can be said to run a risk of loss, who has nothing to start with, and who, therefore, cannot fail to come out from his venture at least as well off as he went in, it is not easy to understand. Only those who have capital can suffer the loss of capital. Therefore, it is they alone who can expose themselves to the chance of loss. Unless, then, we are to limit the term capitalist to those who use their capital in ways involving no more than the minimum amount of risk, the conclusion is unavoidable that the one who assumes a risk to capital is in all cases a capitalist.

It is nearly as self-evident that under normal conditions the person who assumes a risk is the one who will receive the special reward. By what inter-play of economic motives would a capitalist be led to take upon himself the disutility involved in subjecting himself to uncertainty, while surrendering to another the right to the extra product created by his capital because of the uncertainty? No one need expose his capital to more than the minimum degree of risk unless he receives more than the minimum reward for the use of it; therefore, if the economic motive prevails, the assumption of risk and the receipt of the reward for it will be acts of one and the same person. As it is the capitalist who assumes the risk, it is the capitalist who will normally receive the award for risk-taking.

The same fact may be shown more directly by considering the source of the net reward. The attempt has been made in the preceding chapters to prove that the reward for risk-taking is created by the capital exposed to the risk. In a static state every unit of capital will obtain as its reward the part of the product that is specifically imputable to it. Therefore, the owner of the capital that is abnormally productive on account of the risk to which it is exposed will receive the extra product. To claim that this extra product may normally accrue to some one other than the owner of the capital that created it, is to adopt a system of distribution under which some men are able regularly to appropriate wealth created by the capital of others. Such a view is irreconcilable with a productivity theory of distribution, which gives to every agent the product that it creates. It is in this case equally irreconcilable with a sacrifice theory of distribution, since the entire burden of the disutility of risk-taking must evidently be borne by the person who is actually exposed to the possibility of loss.

The net return to capital from a productive operation is economic interest. It is the part of the net product that is created by the capital. It is customary, however, to make a distinction between the product of capital in an industry where competition prevails, and its product in an industry where the capitalist possesses a monopoly advantage. In the latter case, a part of its product is called a monopoly gain, or a monopoly profit. But the difference between the return to capital in the competitive industry and its return in the monopolized one is not a difference in kind. In both cases it receives the part of the product that it creates. It is entirely a question of convenience whether we shall say that the rates of interest are unequal in the two industries, or that the rates of interest are the same and the extra reward is a monopoly profit. In every instance of an abnormally high interest rate, the excess is due to the possession of a monopoly advantage by the owner of the capital. It is important, however, to distinguish between two kinds of monopoly. There is one kind that is founded in the nature of things and another that is artifically created. The capitalist who exposes his capital to risk has a quasi monopoly advantage of the former kind. The obstruction that prevents the free flow of capital into a hazardous investment is not maintained by the owner of the capital already in it. The monopoly is due to the unwillingness of other capitalists to enter the industry. Its effect, unlike that of permanent artificial monopolies, is to promote the best use of capital under existing conditions. The amount of the reward for risk-taking is determined by direct competition, while monopoly profit is determined by the principle of the maximum net revenue.

In the case of capital in hazardous investments, however, as in the case of a true capitalistic monopoly, it is a matter of convenience whether we shall give the name interest to the entire net return to capital, or divide it into two parts and call one pure interest, and the other reward for risk-taking. The important point to notice is that there is no difference in nature between the two incomes. Both are created by capital, and both accrue to the capitalist, and the amount of both is determined on competitive principles. This fundamental unity in the nature of the two incomes seems to be better brought out by applying the term interest to both. We should say, then, that under the influence of risk, capital will be so apportioned in a static state that the rate of interest in different investments will vary with the degree of uncertainty involved in them. In this interest may be distinguished two elements, pure interest, equal in amount to the return to capital in the least hazardous investments,[1] and the reward for risk-taking, the additional return which capital in a more hazardous investment receives.[2]

It is not unusual to divide the gross return to capital, over and above the amount necessary to make good the part regularly used up in productive operations, into pure interest and insurance premium. Here, as before, pure interest is the return to capital in safe investments, but the so-called insurance premium is by no means the same thing as the net reward for risk-taking. The purpose of the insurance premium is the replacement of capital accidentally destroyed. It does not, as a whole, form a part of the net interest on capital. Out of the insurance fund are to be paid all the losses of an uncertain character. Whether the fund will exceed or fall short of the amount necessary to make good the losses cannot be known beforehand, but, as we have already shown, every capitalist will require a large enough gross return on his capital to enable him to set aside an insurance fund in excess of the probable amount of loss as determined by the average of past experience. This excess constitutes the net reward for risk-taking. So, in the case of commercial loans on doubtful security, it would be a mistake to regard the entire excess above the rate on government bonds as net reward for assuming risk. In the absence of other disturbing influences, the reward for risk-taking is the part of the extra return which would be left after deducting an amount large enough to cover the probable loss. It is a matter of common observation that inexperienced investors are apt to be unduly influenced by the apparently high rate of

[1] It may be well to state that all disturbing forces except risk, such as social esteem and difficulty of realizing on an investment, are here left out of consideration. The assumption is that there exists a perfect static adjustment of capital, except for the influence of risk.

It is also necessary to bear in mind the distinction between the capitalistic monopoly mentioned above, in which the possessor of the capital receives the extra product, and an entrepreneur's monopoly, as in the case of the ownership of a patent right, in which the entrepreneur obtains his capital at the market rate and appropriates the extra product.

[2] *Pure* interest, as thus defined, is not to be confounded with *normal,* or *static* interest. The latter is the reward that capital would receive if it were so apportioned that all units of it were equally productive. Pure interest is the reward received in safe investments under an apportionment of capital in which the productivity varies with the uncertainty. Pure interest, therefore, will always be below the static level.

interest in unsafe investments. They do not make sufficient allowance for the losses, the possibility of which is the cause of the high nominal interest. It may be, therefore, that the net return on investments of this kind is below rather than above the return in safe investments. This fact, however, constitutes no exception to the general rule that when risks are properly estimated and appreciated, the net rate of interest will vary in different investments according to the risk involved in them.

That the reward for risk-taking is created by capital and is, therefore, an element of interest, would probably never have been questioned but for the confusion that has resulted from attributing a very complex form of activity to the entrepreneur. It may be worth while to take up directly the question of the relation of the income of the entrepreneur to the reward for risk-taking.

The income of the entrepreneur is called profit. In what sense the term profit must be understood, in order that it may denote an income of a different nature from wages and interest, has been pointed out in the Introduction. In only one respect does it resemble the reward for risk-taking. Both incomes are due to abnormally high productivity in some part of the industrial system—both are quasi monopoly gains. The monopoly advantages in the two cases, however, are not of the same kind. Profit is due to a local and, in a sense, unnatural advantage, which is transient in its character, since it can endure only so long as others are prevented from making use of the device which is the source of the superiority. The reward for risk-taking is due to an advantage the existence of which is founded in the nature of man, and which will endure so long as man's unwillingness to incur risk remains unchanged. Competition will sooner or later annihilate all profit, but it cannot abolish the reward for risk-taking. Profit is a dynamic income; it appears as the result of a dynamic change, and disappears when the inequality in productivity due to the change has induced sufficient movement of capital and labor from group to group. Reward for risk-taking is a static income; it will be present in the approximate static state which alone can be realized while risk exists; other capital will not flow in to cut down the reward to the capital already receiving it, since without the full reward no capital will assume the risk. Profit is a residual income, realized by the sale of the product at a price above the cost of production, and its amount, therefore, cannot be determined until the price is known; reward for risk-taking is a direct income, whose amount is determined by circumstances preceding the sale of the product, just as wages and interest are determined. Reward for risk-taking is a part of the cost of production; profit is the surplus over and above the cost of production.

The attempt to identify the reward for risk-taking with profit runs counter to the obvious fact that there is no uniform relation between the amount of profit and the degree of risk. A large profit may be obtained under conditions involving little or no risk. The gain from the introduction of an improved method of manufacture may be manifest as soon as the improvement is thought of; and the adoption of the new device, while involving no risk, may lead to the appearance of a considerable profit. On the other hand, risk may perfectly well be involved in a form of investment in which no profit is appearing. The manufacture of explosives is an industry in which a fluctuating amount of accidental loss will always be suffered; but in the absence of dynamic changes the possibility of obtaining a profit in that industry would not exist. Indeed, in a dynamic society a profit may be obtained by adopting an improvement whose only purpose is to lessen the chance of uncertain loss, and thus reduce the risk. Such a profit is not the reward for risk-taking, but the result of abolishing risk. Like all other profit it is transient, and will disappear as soon as the improvement has been generally adopted. It is manifest, therefore, that there is no necessary connection between degree of risk and amount of profit.

It has been said that just because profit is a residual income it is an uncertain one, and that it is for the endurance of this uncertainty that the entrepreneur receives his reward. The first statement is obviously not true. As I have already shown, an income is not necessarily uncertain because it is residual. But if that difficulty is overlooked, it is not easy to understand the rest of the statement. We are asked to think of profit as a reward paid to a person for assuming a risk of obtaining no profit. Why should a reward be paid for assuming a risk of which the outcome must be either a gain or no loss? Clearly the incurring of such a risk involves no disutility, and therefore no special inducement is required to assure its assumption. Moreover, even if such a notion were conceivable, it would still be necessary to show a constant relation between the degree of uncertainty as to whether a profit will appear and the size of the profit; and that is as impossible as it is to prove such a relation between profit and risk as ordinarily understood.

The fact that reward for risk-taking is no part of profit, the income of the entrepreneur, may be proved also from the method in which an industry is established. Let us for the sake of simplicity assume an organization of society in which capitalists and entrepreneurs are distinct persons, and in which the entrepreneur performs the organizing and directing work. The capitalists furnish the capital used in the productive operation and receive in return interest, the rate of which is fixed in advance; the entrepreneurs direct and manage the industry, hire the capital and labor, pay all the expenses of production, and receive as their special reward any profit that may be realized. Under such circumstances, will it be the capitalist or the entrepreneur who will obtain the reward for assuming risk?

There are only two ways in which the entrepreneur can realize a net gain because of the existence of risk. He must be able either to obtain his capital at a rate that does not include the reward for assuming risk, or to sell his product at a price higher than is necessary to enable him to pay the reward for risk-taking. Is it possible for him to adopt either of these plans?

As the entrepreneur has no capital to act as a guarantee fund for the capitalist, it is evident that the latter must look to the success of the enterprise for the safety of both principal and interest. He will calculate the risk of loss that he is assuming, and will demand a return in proportion to it. Now the reason why he is able to obtain pure interest on his capital in a safe investment is that the entrepreneur can obtain capital from no one else without paying the interest. Why, then, should he forego the extra reward for risk-taking in a hazardous investment when the entrepreneur must pay the extra reward to any other investor whose capital he may seek to obtain? No economic motive for such conduct can be conceived. The entrepreneur will have to pay for his capital a price proportionate to the risk to which it is to be exposed. Moreover, as we shall see, if capitalists did not demand the extra reward, entrepreneurs would be unable to appropriate any part of it as their own income.

Mangoldt and others have attempted to divide the reward for risk-taking into two parts, and to assign one part to the capitalist and the other to the entrepreneur. A special kind of risk, called by some economic, by others industrial, is said to be assumed by the entrepreneur, and the reward for assuming such risks is either identified with profit or considered to be a part of it. But it seems clear that there can be no ground for such a distinction, on our assumption of a complete separation of the functions of entrepreneur and capitalist. As the entrepreneur has nothing to lose, it is impossible for him to assume a risk of any kind; and as the capitalist bears the entire risk, there is no reason why he should be any more willing to suffer loss in one way than in another. It is all one to him whether he loses his capital through a technical failure or an industrial one. It is not reasonable to suppose that he would demand a consideration for assuming the risk of loss in one way and gratuitously assume a risk of another kind. Finally, if all capitalists did act in that uneconomic way, it would be impossible, as I shall show presently, for the entrepreneur to obtain any extra gain on account of the industrial risk.

It seems clear, then, that as no capitalist will incur a risk of any kind unless he is rewarded for it, no entrepreneur can obtain capital without paying a price proportionate to the risk to which it is to be exposed. Does the existence of risk make it any more possible for him to obtain a price for his product that will leave him a net gain? In the long run the price he can get is determined by the expense of production. Only when he is obtaining a higher price is he realizing a profit. The existence of such a profit in any part of the industrial system is an invitation to other entrepreneurs to come in and share it. If, then, we assume that an entrepreneur who is using capital in a hazardous industry is obtaining a price for his product that leaves him a net profit after paying for his labor and capital, with the reward for risk-taking included, it is clear that such a profit would soon be annihilated by the competition of other entrepreneurs.

The same thing would happen to the extra gain that an entrepreneur would realize if capitalists as a class should suddenly become willing to forego the reward for assuming either all kinds of risk or a special kind. The necessity of exposing capital to the chance of loss can have no terrors for the entrepreneur, since the loss will not fall upon him, but upon the capitalist. If, then, all capitalists consent to assume risks for nothing, all entrepreneurs will be able to obtain capital for purposes involving risks at a lower rate than they formerly paid; and the competition of entrepreneurs with one another will prevent any one of them from keeping the price of the product above the level that his reduced expense justifies. If capitalists incur risks without any extra inducement, it will be consumers, and not entrepreneurs, who will benefit by their forbearance.

For the entrepreneur the reward for risk-taking is an element in the cost of production. The price of a commodity in whose creation risk is involved is higher than it would be if the risk were absent. The gross return to the entrepreneur is greater. The entire excess, however, due to the existence of risk, he has to hand over to the capitalist; for the amount of the extra return that he can secure on account of the risk is fixed by the extra interest that he is compelled to pay for his capital.

The most consistent attempt that has been made to identify entrepreneur's profit with the reward for risk-taking is that of Mr. Hawley.[3] Many of the arguments with which he defends his position have been considered in the comparison already made between the two forms of income; but there is at the basis of his contention a misconception concerning the significance of the term productivity as applied to the assumption of risk, to which it may be well to devote a little attention. It is most clearly brought out in the following passages. Professor Clark, he says, "acknowledging that the reward of risk-carrying exists and has hitherto escaped recognition, and that it constitutes a peculiar form of income, . . . refuses to accompany me in identifying it with profit, and claims that the reward of enterprise inures to the capitalist as such, and not to the entrepreneur as such, thus making the capitalist unique among producers, in that he alone enjoys two quite distinct forms of income, the one springing from the use and the other from the venturing of the capital, but

[3] Frederick G. Hawley: "The Risk Theory of Profit," *Quarterly Journal of Economics,* vol. vii, p. 459.

both accruing to him in his peculiar industrial function." "It is not of course impossible," he continues, "that the exercise of a single function may be followed by two *radically* distinct classes of results. But it appears to me as an axiom of scientific method, that two *radically* distinct classes of results shall not be ascribed to the same function as their source." And yet again: "According to Professor Clark, if I rightly comprehend him, we have in economics a problem of four forces, producing five distinct classes of results—land yielding rent, labor yielding wages, capital yielding interest and reward for risk, and coördination (if he will allow me to so name the force) yielding profit."

In spite of the ambiguity involved in Mr. Hawley's use of the term "enterprise" to denote the activity of the entrepreneur, we seem to be justified in inferring that according to his idea it is by virtue of his assumption of risk that the entrepreneur obtains a profit, and that the reason for distinguishing the reward for risk-taking from interest, and assigning it to a separate productive agent, is to be found in the necessity of assuming distinct functions as the sources of "*radically* distinct classes of results." Now it may be "an axiom of scientific method that two *radically* distinct classes of results shall not be ascribed to the same function as their source," but the principle has no application in the present case. There is no such difference in the natures of the two incomes, interest and reward for risk-taking, as Mr. Hawley seems to imagine. I have already shown that risk-taking is productive only in a secondary sense; it increases the productivity of capital. Capital creates the reward for risk-taking, and receives it as a part of its net income. It receives a higher rate of interest in a hazardous investment than in a safe one, but the additional return differs in no essential respect from the minimum return, to which the term pure interest is applied.

Mr. Hawley proposes to put in a separate category of distribution the excess of interest that capital receives as the result of assuming risk. If he should follow his method of analysis to its logical conclusion, he would have to treat in the same way every other excessive increment in the return to capital. Risk is not the only thing that prevents the static apportionment of capital. Social odium, for example, may have the same result. If the investment of capital in any kind of business brings with it loss of public esteem, an abnormally high return will be necessary to induce capital to enter it. The marginal productivity of capital in the industry will be above the static level, and the rate of interest will be correspondingly high. But Mr. Hawley would hardly be willing to carry out the principle he has laid down and regard the incurring of social odium as a separate economic function, creating and receiving a radically distinct share of product. There is no more reason for making such a distinction in the case of the abnormally high interest that capital receives as a reward for incurring risk.[4]

We have seen that the attempt to identify reward for risk-taking with entrepreneur's profit is based on a misconception of the nature of the two incomes, and that the recognition of this reward as a separate category of distribution cannot be justified on the ground that the reward is created by a distinct economic agent. But the suggestion has been made[5] that it might be well for other reasons to give that form of income an independent place in the scheme of distribution. Without stopping to consider the arguments that have been advanced in favor of such a course, I may mention two or three that seem to me to be conclusive against it.

If the new category were to include the extra reward that labor sometimes obtains in dangerous occupations, as well as the extra reward of capital, it would be found impossible to make much practical use of it, on account of the different principles by which the two rewards are determined. Moreover the inclusion of a part of wages and a part of interest in one group would cut across the classes already recognized, and seriously impair the significance of the classification.

If, on the other hand, it is proposed to have the new category include only the extra reward that accrues to capital on account of risk, the objections to the plan are no less weighty. In the first place it is inexpedient. It places the emphasis on the points of unlikeness between pure interest and the reward for risk-taking, when it is more important to bring out their essential likeness.

[4] Mr. Hawley's classification of incomes fails to make any disposition of profit, as the term is here used. It is not a part of wages or of interest, and if the preceding argument is sound, it by no means corresponds to the reward for risk-taking.

[5] T. N. Carver, "The Place of Abstinence in the Theory of Interest," *Quarterly Journal of Economics*, vol. viii, p. 58, note.

Clear economic thinking will be promoted by establishing the distinction between the reward for risk-taking and profit, and in no way can that be better accomplished than by showing the identity of the former income with interest. In the second place it is unscientific. It completely destroys the coördination of the classification. To divide incomes into profit, wages, interest, and the reward for risk-taking, is much like dividing material bodies into inanimate objects, plants, animals, and men. There are reasons why it is important to distinguish the reward for risk-taking from other interest, just as there are reasons for distinguishing men from other animals; but to make a separate and distinct class out of a subdivision of a class already recognized is to do violence to scientific method.

Wages, interest and profit are independent, exhaustive, and mutually exclusive forms of income. Reward for risk-taking may be a part of wages or it may be a part of interest; it has no independent standing, and therefore it has no claim to rank as a coördinate category of distribution. It is best to abide by the existing classification of incomes, and to think of rates of wages or of interest as varying in different employments under the influence of risk.

In the present chapter we have attempted to show that the reward for risk-taking is neither the whole nor any part of profit, and therefore does not accrue to the entrepreneur; that it is a part of interest and accrues in all cases to the capitalist; and that it is inexpedient and unscientific to make it an independent category of distribution, coördinate with wages, interest and profit.

CHAPTER VI

WAYS OF MEETING RISK

Up to this point in our discussion we have proceeded as if the degree of risk involved in any enterprise were an unchangeable quantity, which the investor must in all cases assume if he decides to enter the industry. As a matter of fact, however, the degree of risk may be changed by the conduct of the investor himself. The adoption of devices for lessening the chances of accidental loss, and for diminishing the unfavorable influence of uncertainty, is one of the most important forms of progress in a dynamic society. How much risk would be involved in different industries in the approximate static state, and how much deterrent effect a given degree of risk would have on investors of capital, would depend on the stage of economic development that the society had reached before dynamic changes ceased. We must now turn our attention to a consideration of the devices that have been adopted by society to counteract the unfavorable influence of risk. Some of these may be carried out by an individual investor; others require the combined action of two or more men, and are there-fore of a social nature. We will begin with those that do not require social cooperation.

A man living in isolation may carry on certain productive operations and accumulate a limited stock of capital goods. Let us imagine that he has cleared a piece of land and fashioned tools with which to work it. On half of the land he is able to raise all of some crop, as potatoes, that he cares for; he is con-sidering whether he shall raise corn or tobacco on the other half. The circumstances on which his decision depends are these: He would much rather have a crop of tobacco than a crop of corn; the cost in labor and in wear and tear of his capital is the same in the two cases, if he cultivates the tobacco in the easiest way; but there is considerably more uncertainty about the size of the tobacco crop than about that of the corn crop. Under such conditions it is evident that his choice between tobacco and corn will depend on the relation between the excess of the utility of the tobacco over that of the corn, and the disutility of the uncertainty about the amount of tobacco he will obtain.

It may be that the uncertainty in the case of the tobacco can be diminished by a change in the method of cultivation. Let us suppose that it is due to the occasional failure of a crop on account of prolonged drought. It may be possible to adopt measures to guard against the loss. If the tobacco is to be raised, any change in the method of cultivation that lessens the chance of loss without increasing the cost in labor and capital will evidently be adopted. If the tobacco would suffer less on that part of the land where the potatoes had been raised, while the latter would do as well on one part as on the other, the change of location of the two crops would certainly be made. If, on the other hand, the method of counteracting the effect of the drought involved additional cost, the decision as to the advisability of adopting it would not be so easy to reach. It might be possible by a system of irrigation to lessen or even to annihilate the danger of loss from drought; but the introduction of such a system would involve more or less additional cost. On what principle would the choice be made between the two possible methods of cultivation? It would evidently be by a comparison of disutilities. The disutility of the additional sacrifice incidental to the introduction of the system of irrigation would be set over against the disutility of the uncertainty involved in raising the tobacco without artificial irrigation. If the former were less than the latter, irrigation would be adopted; if it were greater, the danger of accidental loss would be borne.

A man in isolation, then, face to face with unequal degrees of risk involved in different ways of using his capital and labor, is restricted to three possible modes of conduct. He may avoid the uncertainty peculiar to a specific form of industrial activity by keeping out of the industry; he may reduce the degree of uncertainty by adopting devices that make the occurrence of the loss less probable; or he may assume the risk and endure the attendant uncertainty. The first form of activity may be called avoidance of risk, the second, prevention, and the last, assumption. It is possible to combine the second and third methods by partially eliminating the risk through preventive measures and assuming the rest of it. The choice between different possible modes of action will be determined by a comparison of the disutilities involved in going without the product of the hazardous industry, in using the additional labor and capital necessary to reduce the risk, and in enduring the uncertainty incidental to the creation of the product.

A man living in society has the same opportunity of making a selection between the three ways of meeting risk, and his choice is determined by a similar comparison of utilities and disutilities. These, however, are not of precisely the same nature as those which the man in isolation compares. The commodities created by different producers are not intended for the immediate satisfaction of the wants of those who create them; they are produced for exchange. It is no longer possible, therefore, for the person who produces a commodity to make a direct comparison between its utility to the consumer of it and the disutility involved in creating it. Confining our attention now to the risks incurred in the employment of capital, let us see in what way the utilities in question are determined.

The choice between safe and unsafe investments turns on the relative risks and rates of interest in the two investments and on the unwillingness of the investor to incur risk. If the extra return to be expected in the unsafe investment is large enough to offset the reluctance of the investor to incur the risk, he will choose that investment. He compares the utility of the probable increase in income with the disutility of the uncertainty.

We have already noted that the reluctance to incur risk is not the same in all men. This fact has an important influence upon the assumption of risk in a catallactic society. Those who are most unwilling to take any chances naturally seek the safest investments, and those whose reluctance is least find their advantage in entering hazardous industries. The utility of the additional gain to be realized in such investments more than offsets for them the disutility of the uncertainty. If there were enough investors of all degress of unwillingness, so that the unwillingness always varied inversely as the risk, the entire cost of inequalities in risk would be annihilated. But evidently such is not the case. There is a disproportionate amount of capital in safe investments. It is true, however, that on account of this adaptation of investors to risks, the reward to be obtained for assuming risk does not always increase in proportion to the risk. The selection of the more hazardous investments by those who are least reluctant to assume risk reduces the net cost of risk to society.

The choice between a safe and an unsafe investment, then, is determined by the subjective estimates put by the investor upon the utility of the increased income in the hazardous investment and the disutility of the uncertainty. As the decision thus depends upon subjective factors, it is impossible to prophesy how any particular investor will act. The choice between different methods of carrying on an industry, that is, the question as to the adoption of any preventive measure, is determined in the first instance in much the same way. Comparison is made between the disutility involved in investing the additional capital necessary to introduce the preventive measure, and the disutility of the greater uncertainty if such a measure is not introduced. But here it is evident that the choice is not left entirely at the discretion of the investor. It is only when the interest on the capital required to introduce the preventive measure just equals the extra price necessary to bring about the assumption of the risk if the preventive measure is not introduced, that it is optional with an entrepreneur which method he shall adopt. If one method makes it possible to produce a commodity with less expense than the óther involves, that method, in the absence of disturbing influences, will finally become universal. Therefore in the end it is by a comparison of the relative expenses that the choice between the different methods will be determined. All preventive measures will be adopted that do not involve as much expense as would be incurred on account of the necessity of paying capital for the assumption of the risk that the measures are intended to annihilate.

It is easy to see that in a dynamic society the possibility of realizing a profit by first using a preventive device that reduces expense is a great incentive to progress in the technique of production. It would be a mistake, however, to suppose that progress must always be in the direction of reducing risk. The reward for risk-taking is only one element in the cost of production. If the adoption of a more uncertain method of creating a commodity made possible a considerable reduction in the amount of the capital and labor employed, it might cause the appearance of a profit. There would be less danger of destruction of property if the speed of trains were limited to ten miles an hour. The gain in other directions from the increased speed, however, more than counterbalances the effect of the greater uncertainty about the amount of loss. Whenever the additional expense caused by the increase in uncertainty is less than the saving due to the increased productivity of labor and capital, a profit may be realized by inaugurating the more uncertain method of production.

A person living in a society where production is carried on for the purpose of exchange, and where all sorts of personal relationships are established, is exposed to different risks from those which threaten a man in isolation. Some forms of static risk are reduced through the existence of society; others are greatly increased; while all those connected with the relations established between different men exist only in society. Special social institutions, such as the credit system, introduce many peculiar chances of loss and greatly increase the uncertainty of economic life. Dynamic risks are even more affected. A man living in isolation, producing solely for his own consumption, is not entirely free from risk of this kind. There may be a change in his disposition so that he ceases to care for a commodity of which he has accumulated a store; or he may make a discovery or an invention which renders useless a capital good that he has created. One who is producing commodities for exchange, however, is evidently subjected to far greater chances of dynamic loss. It may befall him on account of his failure to anticipate changes in the wants of distant consumers; or it may be due to an invention made by any one of a thousand competing producers. Another form of dynamic risk appears only in society, namely, uncertainty as to the action of governments on such questions as taxation, franchises, property rights, and the like. While, therefore, it is undoubtedly true that what may be called *natural* risk, uncertainty connected with the direct relations between man and nature, is much reduced by the development of a social state, society brings with itself a large class of distinctly *social* risks, resulting from the relations established between different human beings, which far exceed in number and variety the risks of the isolated state.

On the other hand, society does much to assist the individual in warding off many forms of loss. Armies and navies, judges, magistrates, sheriffs, and policemen are supported largely for the purpose of preventing loss through violence or fraud. Information of various kinds is collected and disseminated by the government to assist its citizens in forming correct judgments as to the future movements of prices. There is a cordon of life-saving stations to lessen the dangers of the sea, and a weather bureau to give warning of the approach of unfavorable climatic conditions. Cities and towns support fire services to reduce the danger of conflagrations and to limit their destructiveness. Education is intended to increase honesty and carefulness as well as knowledge and ability.

The state goes even further than this. It compels its citizens to do some things and to refrain from doing others, when such regulations are necessary to protect other persons from the chance of loss. A man having knowledge of an intended robbery must give warning to the proper authorities; within specific limits no one is allowed to erect a wooden building; the manufacture and storage of explosives in thickly settled communities is frequently restricted. In many ways the freedom of the citizen is limited for the purpose of warding off injury to the property of others.

It is not alone through its official organs that society seeks to guard the security of its members. The same object is sought through voluntary associations of many varieties. There are combinations of manufacturers, wholesale dealers, retailers, real-estate owners, bankers, members of professions and of trades, inhabitants of sections of cities or of county districts, and countless others, that exist, wholly or in part, to protect those who belong to them from various kinds of loss. Finally, other forms of preventive activity are carried on by individuals for the purpose of private gain. A trade journal is partly supported by those who wish to reach correct judgments about existing industrial conditions by means of the information the paper contains, and thus lessen the danger of mistakes in the quantity and quality of the commodities they produce. The chief benefit of a mercantile agency is the protection it affords against the unwise extension of credit. The development of cheap and rapid means of communication has done much to reduce the amount of dynamic risk. On the one hand, it makes it possible to secure early information about industrial changes in distant places, and on the other hand, it enables a surplus of commodities in any limited area to be distributed throughout society. It has also led to the development of a special trade custom, which has reduced the dynamic risk connected with the production of many articles. To a great and increasing extent commodities are now manufactured "to order," and the danger of piling up large stocks for which no market can be obtained is thus avoided.

These facts, and many others of a similar character which will occur to the reader, indicate the great importance that is attached to the prevention of accidental loss and the reduction of the amount of uncertainty. Every such device substitutes a definite expense of production for the chance of an indefinite loss. So far as the nature of the expense is concerned, it is a matter of indifference whether the preventive measure is carried out by individuals, by private associations, or by public bodies. Its distribution among these different agencies depends upon considerations of relative cost and efficiency. The question of the adoption of any such device is determined by a comparison of the relative costs of the device and of the uncertainty it is intended to annihilate. The statement sometimes made that as far as possible all accidental loss is prevented, is true only in a modified sense. It is easy to see that much more could be done to make such losses impossible. For instance, farmers might build their barns of fireproof material, or burglary might be almost entirely prevented by a sufficient increase in the number of policemen. The correct statement would be that everything is done that can be done economically. It would be poor economy for society, for the purpose of preventing accidental loss, to use up deliberately more capital than would be destroyed by the event whose occurrence is dreaded. The tendency will be to adopt every preventive device which in the end yields a net gain to society; and the practical test will be found in the comparative cost of producing the commodities by the more and the less uncertain methods.

It may be worth while to consider whether the self interest of entrepreneurs can be relied upon to insure the adoption of all preventive measures which are economically desirable for society.

It is evident that this is not the case when the measure is one whose adoption has been made compulsory by law. If one builder could avoid expense by substituting a somewhat inflammable material for the fireproof material that his neighbors and competitors are compelled to use, his risk of loss by fire would not be increased in proportion to the reduction in his expense. It is sometimes said, however, that there is a more fundamental opposition than this between public and private interests, and that it may at times be necessary for society to compel the adoption of preventive measures which individual entrepreneurs would have no incentive for introducing. Let us assume that an industry has been carried on under conditions that allowed a fluctuating amount of loss. The commodity produced in that industry will then be selling at a price which in a series of years will make good the loss to the group as a whole, and give each investor an extra reward on account of the risk he has been carrying. Let us suppose further that by the adoption of some preventive measure the average amount of accidental loss and the extent of the fluctuations could both be reduced. The improvement would evidently be adopted by individual entrepreneurs unless the expense of it was so great that the commodity could not be sold at as low a price as it was before. If it did involve an increase in price, would it under any circumstances be to the economic advantage of society to have it adopted? It appears not. It is true that the improvement would prevent the accidental destruction of a certain amount of capital, and would also cut down the amount of the extra reward for risk-taking; but that saving could be accomplished only by the deliberate destruction of a greater amount of capital to prevent the occurrence of the accidental loss. It appears clear, therefore, that under conditions of free competition the adoption by individual entrepreneurs of any preventive measure that is for the economic advantage of society will be assured by the possibilty of obtaining a profit as a result of introducing it.[1]

[1] In the absence of any system of insurance, legal compulsion may be justified in two classes of cases, namely: when the economic loss of the individual is liable to be accompanied by physical or mental injury to others, and when it is apt to cause loss of property by those who are unable to protect themselves. Laws prescribing the use of fireproof material in dwelling houses in thickly settled communities may be justified in either way.

We have been considering the social aspect of the three ways of meeting risk that are common to men in isolation and to those in society. We have called them respectively avoidance, prevention and assumption. We must now notice other courses of action, which are possible only in society. These are distribution, transfer and combination of risks. That these different methods of meeting risk are by no means mutually exclusive will be manifest as we proceed. We will consider each of them in turn.

If ten men each put $1000 into a hazardous investment, the risk may be said to be distributed. If a loss occurs it will be partially borne by each of the ten men. We have already noted that under the influence of the law of diminishing utility an investor's reluctance to expose a given amount of capital to a definite risk decreases as his wealth increases. In general, we may say that the smaller the ratio is between the sum to be risked and the person's entire capital, the less is the reluctance to expose it to risk. If, then, the capital for a hazardous industry is made up of the marginal increments of the capital of many investors, the amount necessary to induce them to incur the risk will be less than the reward that would be necessary to induce a single investor in the same economic circumstances to advance the entire amount. The superiority of the corporate form of industry is partly due to this fact.[2] It brings together the marginal increments of the capital of many investors. That it possesses many other great advantages goes without saying; but we are concerned only with its relation to the assumption of risk. In a dynamic society it creates the possibility of making many industrial experiments which no individual investor would care to undertake. In a static society the prevalence of the corporate form of industry lowers the expense of producing commodities by reducing the reluctance to incur risk and the amount paid for its assumption. On account of the limited liability of the members of corporations this gain is partially offset by an increase in the risk of those who become creditors of the corporation. On the other hand, the very limitation of liability greatly reduces the reluctance of the members of the corporation to incur risk. The net result is undoubtedly a very considerable gain to society in

[2] J. B. Clark, "Insurance and Business Profit," *Quarterly Journal of Economics*, vol. vii, p. 52.

the form of a cheapening of commodities, made possible by the reduction in the amount paid to capital for assuming risk.

A second method of distributing risk is the mutual guarantee against loss, sometimes entered into by a number of producers exposed to the same danger. This form of combination is too familiar to need any lengthy description. It is generally known as mutual insurance. In some cases the mutual guarantee is attended with the accumulation of a surplus, in others it is not. As the introduction of a surplus brings with it certain consequences which must be left for later consideration, we will for the present confine our attention to the effect of the guarantee alone. By such a guarantee all the members of a combination pledge themselves to make good a loss of some specified kind which befalls any one of them. The payments of each member are determined partly by the amount of loss that actually occurs and partly by the value of the property insured by him. It is evident that, on the assumption that the amount of positive loss is not affected by the existence of the combination, such an arrangement will reduce the cost of risk to society. There is a substitution of a large chance of a small loss each year for a small chance of a large loss. Now the unfavorable consequences of a loss increase out of proportion to the increase in the amount of the loss; and therefore, while the amount of the probable loss for a series of years is not affected by a mutual guarantee, the reluctance of the producers to assume the chance of such loss is diminished. There will be, therefore, a reduction in the price of the products of the industries affected. It must be borne in mind that the gain realized by society through the devices that we are considering is not due to any diminution in the amount of capital actually destroyed. A mutual guarantee against loss need not in any way affect the amount of positive loss. Whatever social gain is made is entirely due to the diminution of the negative loss which the existence of risk entails. Any device that lessens the unwillingness of men to incur risk brings the apportionment of capital nearer to the ideal static standard and thus increases its productivity. It is the increased product thus created that constitutes the social gain.

There is another economic advantage in the mutual guarantee against loss, which is due to the combination of a number of risks in a group and the consequent reduction of the degree of uncertainty for the group as a whole. This is the third of the social devices for meeting risk, the discussion of which must be postponed to the following chapter. We will now turn our attention to the second device, the transfer of risk.

If one person guarantees another against possible accidental loss of any kind, there is a transfer of the risk of such loss from the latter person to the former. When the transaction takes place between persons who estimate risk alike, and who are equally reluctant to assume it, it will not occur without a simultaneous transfer of the reward to be obtained for carrying the risk. There would be no social gain in such an operation. If, however, the person who assumes the risk is for any reason less reluctant to do so than the one from whom it is transferred, the price paid for the transfer may be fixed somewhere between the reward demanded by the latter and the minimum amount which the former would require. There is an opportunity for both parties to the transaction to realize a net gain. The one to whom it is transferred obtains a reward for carrying it in excess of the amount that would be necessary to induce him to assume it; and the one who transfers it purchases security at a price that does not take from him the entire net reward for risk-taking in the industry in which his capital is invested. Both of these gains are profits. The competition of the less reluctant risk-takers will gradually cut down the price that can be obtained for assuming the risks to an amount that just compensates the marginal member of the group; and on the other hand, if all investors in the hazardous enterprise can find risk-takers who will relieve them of uncertainty for a lower reward than they themselves demand, there will be an influx of capital into the industry which will sooner or later bring down the price of the product to the level that the reduced expense justifies. When the new adjustment has been reached, the productivity of capital will have been increased and society benefited.

Now it is a matter of common observation that men differ greatly, both in their confidence in their own judgment about the chance of loss and in their willingness to assume chances that they estimate alike. There is in consequence a differentiation of the owners of capital into two classes according to their attitude towards risk. To the more enterprising class, anxious for industrial control, and willing to incur the incidental risks, President Hadley gives the name speculators.[3] The others may in contrast

3 Arthur Twining Hadley, *Economics*, New York, 1896, p. 112. The influence of risk occupies so prominent a place in President Hadley's discussion of distribution that it seems necessary to give his treatment of it special attention. It is not easy, however, to determine just what his position is. On the one hand, there is no separate discussion of the theory of risk, and on the other, it is sometimes difficult to reconcile statements concerning risks, made in different connections. The entire net return to capital he calls gross profits. Their amount is determined in the following way: "The competition of capitalists with one another leads them to advance to the laborers a sum equal to the expected price of the product, less a compensation for waiting and the risks attendant upon it, sufficient to induce the proprietors to hazard the required amount of capital" (p. 300). Here gross profits seem to be regarded as reward for waiting and for risk-taking. Many of his statements, however, do not refer specifically to the waiting, and therefore seem, in form at least, to attribute gross profits to risk-taking alone. Thus on p. 265: "In fact, they [capitalists] will not wish to go so far as this point [*Or*]; for at *Or* they simply recover what they advance [to laborers in the form of wages], with no compensation for the risks which are always involved. To assume these risks they must have some adequate motive." Yet we find (p. 267) gross profits divided as follows:

1. "A payment for *capital* known as *interest*.
2. "A payment for *location* known as *rent*.
3. "A payment for *skill* known as *net profit*."

"The separation of interest from net profit or rent results in a separation of the reward for waiting from the rewards for risk and foresight" (p. 300). The last sentence seems to mean that interest is the reward for waiting, net profit for risk-taking, and rent for foresight. It is not easy to understand exactly how the same income can be at once reward for skill and reward for risk-taking. Skill and the assumption of risk are by no means universally correlated. But we are still further confused when we find from other passages that interest and rent are also affected by risk. As to interest: "This rate [of interest on what is considered absolutely good security] is not looked at by the individual as a payment for risk. Yet its height is probably in large measure a result of past experience as to losses" (p. 280, note). As to rent: "Economic rent and net profit are like the producers' and consumers' surplus . . . in being differential gains. . . . They are unlike them . . . in being affected by differential losses which in some instances more than neutralize the gains. . . . But in point of fact, both rent and profits are of the nature of compensation for risk" (p. 288). It thus appears that all forms of income except wages are more or less "of the nature of compensation for risk." It is not thought possible, however, to correlate the income of the individual with the risk he runs. "Many of the writers who treat of the relation between business risk and business profit make the mistake of assuming that profits are an amount paid to the individual capitalist to cover *his* risk of loss. Far from it. They are paid to capitalists as a class for protecting the public against *its* risk of loss" (p. 288).

One fact stands out clearly in all of President Hadley's references to "compensation for risk." The income to which he applies that term is not at all the same as that which we have identified as the special reward for assuming risk. What he has in mind is the chance gain of those capitalists who are so fortunate as to escape disaster. It is that sum which he connects with the skill of the investors, and which he is naturally unable to correlate with the amount of risk they run. Nowhere does he appear to recognize the existence of the net reward for assuming risk. As he definitely rejects productivity and be called investors. The class of investors embraces those capitalists who for any reason are chiefly concerned with obtaining a sure income, even if the amount of it is small; the class of speculators consists of those who are so powerfully attracted by the possibility of securing large gains, that they are willing to assume the chance of suffering accidental losses. Of course no hard-and-fast line can be drawn between the two classes. Degrees of risk and degrees of unwillingness to incur risk increase from the lowest to the highest by infinitesimal increments. In a general way, however, the two types of capitalists can be readily distinguished.

Of the effect of this difference in character on the direct assumption of risk we have already spoken; we are now concerned only with the system of transfer of risk which it makes possible. Venturesome capitalists are evidently the ones who will be most likely to assume exceptional risks. They may be attracted either by the exceptionally large reward for assuming risk, or by the hope of realizing a profit. They constitute the class of capitalist-entrepreneurs, whose peculiar relation to risk must now be considered.[4] It has already been shown that an entrepreneur with no capital of his own must pay for capital a price proportional to the risk to which it is to be exposed. Reward for risk-taking is no part of his income. On the other hand, a capitalist-entrepreneur who uses no capital except his own will receive as his income the entire net product of the industry in excess of the amount paid for the labor he hires. It would be difficult to distinguish practically between his interest, with the reward for assuming risk included, and his profit. There is a special complication, however, in those cases where the entrepreneur makes use both of his own capital and of borrowed capital in the same venture. It is the effect of this combination of capital that we are to consider.

The relation between the capitalist-entrepreneur and the persons from whom he obtains his additional capital are affected

---

sacrifice as determinants of the reward to capital, and as it is, so far as man's knowledge is concerned, uncertain which of two equally able and cautious investors will escape accidental loss of capital, it is evident that the influence of chance fills a very large place in President Hadley's theory.

4 J. B. Clark, "Insurance and Business Profit," *Quarterly Journal of Economics,* vol. vii, p. 47, *et seq.*

by the following facts: The capitalist-entrepreneur generally has a large part of his capital invested in the industry that he is managing, while his borrowed capital may consist of the marginal units of several investors. The desire of capitalists for a reasonable assurance of the safety of their capital leads them to limit the amount that they will lend to the capitalist-entrepreneur. The latter is generally personally liable for all loss and indebtedness, while the possible loss of the other investors cannot exceed their actual investment. Finally, it is seldom that an industrial venture results in total loss; and in case of partial loss the capitalist-entrepreneur has to bear it all, unless it exceeds the total amount of his own capital. Under such conditions it is evident that, while all the capital is used in the same industry, it is not all exposed to the same degree of risk. The capitalist-entrepreneur has assumed practically all the risk. The other capitalists have made a transfer of the risk to which their capital would naturally have been exposed in the industry in question. Consequently they demand only a small reward in excess of pure interest for incurring the small risk which they still bear. While the degree of risk to which the industry as a whole is exposed remains unchanged, and the capitalist-entrepreneur may, therefore, be able to obtain a large extra reward on account of the risk, he is obliged to hand over to the other capitalists little or none of this extra gain. It becomes a part of his own income.

It is important to notice that this part of the capitalist-entrepreneur's income is not profit. It accrues to the capitalist, and not to the entrepreneur. Because the capital of the capitalist-entrepreneur is exposed to a high degree of risk, it is able to obtain a high rate of reward. If the income were profit, it would be annihilated by the competition of other capitalist-entrepreneurs. They would obtain capital on the same terms, and cut down the price of the commodity to the point where it would yield only so much extra income as it was necessary for them to pay to the other capitalists for the slight risk that the latter still ran. But capitalist-entrepreneurs will not act in that way. Their own capital is exposed to a high degree of risk, and they will not be willing to assume it without adequate reward. Their competition will reduce the price of the commodity only to the point where it yields them in addition to pure interest a net income that is just enough to reward them for assuming the risk. This income is determined directly, just as pure interest is, and its amount is fixed by the reluctance of the capitalist-entrepreneurs to expose their capital to risk.

As we have already stated, the transfer of risk does not necessarily reduce the degree of risk. The danger that actually threatens the capital in an industry may be in no way affected by the fact that the risk is disproportionally borne. At the same time, the cost of risk must be in some way reduced by the transfer, if there is to be any social gain from the transaction. The capitalist-entrepreneur must be willing to bear the risk that is transferred to him by other capitalists for a smaller reward than they would demand, if they managed the business themselves. This greater readiness to enter a hazardous industry may be due to the hope of large gains from sources not open to the other capitalists, or it may be due to differences in personal character. In a dynamic society the former influence is frequently predominant. It is sometimes the possibility of realizing a large temporary profit from a successful industrial venture, and not the amount of the reward for risk-taking, that makes the capitalist-entrepreneur willing to assume a high degree of risk for a small reward. In a static society, however, it is evident that any social gain that may be obtained through this form of organization must be due to differences in the character of different capitalists. On the one hand, those of a more venturesome disposition will be less reluctant to assume risk, and therefore will be found in the more exposed positions. On the other hand, if the capitalist-entrepreneur possesses, along with the venturesomeness, greater skill in calculating risk, and readiness in devising expedients for avoiding danger, than the other capitalists, the result of the transfer will be an actual reduction of the risk. Because the risk which the capitalist-entrepreneur assumes is less than that to which the other capitalists would be exposed if they were managing the business, the entrepreneur is willing to assume the risk of the industry for a smaller reward than the others would demand. The outcome will be a differentiation of capitalists according to their fitness for different kinds of service. Those who are especially reluctant to incur risk, and those who are poorly adapted to manage hazardous industries, will put their capital into positions of comparative safety; those who should occupy the exposed positions on account of their peculiar fitness for doing so, will assume the large risks incidental to the performance of the function of the capitalist-entrepreneur. Society will be benefited by the arrangement, as it is by all forms of division of labor that result in securing the right man for the right place. So far as the influence of risk is concerned, the gain will be measured by the reduction in the cost of commodities due to the actual diminution of the risk and to the lowering of the reward necessary to induce the assumption of risk.

There is a point of special importance in connection with this peculiar income of the capitalist-entrepreneur that must not be left unmentioned. It is commonly said that according to the productivity theory of distribution each unit of capital in a static state receives as its reward the part of the net product that is specifically imputable to it. It may be asked, then, in what sense the capital of the capitalist-entrepreneur is more productive than the rest of the capital in the same industry. It is evident that all the capital, after it has been put into an industry, contributes equally to the creation of the physical product. The capital of the entrepreneur, however, renders an additional service; it insures the capital of the other investors. The answer to the question here raised, therefore, evidently depends on the answer to the more general question, in what sense capital is productive whose only service is the creation of security. As it will be more convenient to consider that question in connection with the subject of insurance, we shall postpone our discussion of it to the following chapter.

We have examined in the present chapter the three ways of meeting risk that are common to men in isolation and to men in society, calling them respectively avoidance, prevention and assumption. The attempt has been made to discover on what principle the choice between them would be determined by a man in isolation, and how the application of this principle is affected by the existence of society, and by a system of production for exchange. Two essentially social methods of meeting risk have also been considered. These are the distribution of risk, realized by the corporate form of industry, and by the system of mutual guarantee against loss, and the transfer of risk, one form of which is seen in the capitalist-entrepreneur mode of organization. It remains to examine another device, which combines the two social methods already noticed and the third method, to which we have referred as the combination of risks. In the next chapter we shall discuss the economic significance of insurance in a static society.

CHAPTER VII

INSURANCE

The term insurance has already been used in describing the fund accumulated to meet uncertain losses. It is evident that in a static state all producers who are exposed to risk must accumulate such funds. While it is uncertain whether the accumulation of any individual producer will be enough to meet the loss he suffers, that of the entire body of producers in any industry must be large enough to cover the losses of the group as a whole. Otherwise there would be in the long run a great diminution in the amount of capital in hazardous industries, and a serious disturbance of the static adjustment. Such a phenomenon is inconsistent with the notion of the static state. A fruit-dealer who at irregular intervals suffers loss through decay must add to the price of his fruit enough to cover such uncertain loss. A ship-owner has to increase his freight rates more or less, if his ships occasionally lie idle in port. In this sense, then, every producer, in the absence of all opportunity of transferring his risk, must insure himself. Such insurance would be defined as the accumulation of a fund to meet uncertain losses. From the point of view of economic theory, as has already been shown, the insurance fund includes only that part of the accumulation that is intended to cover the uncertain part of the loss; it is that part only whose amount is affected by the influence of uncertainty.

This individualistic method of providing for uncertain loss is spoken of sometimes as *latent* insurance,[1] and sometimes as *self*-insurance. The latter term is usually applied to such conduct on the part of large concerns with many risks of kinds commonly

[1] "Partout où il y a un risque à courir, une assurance latente protège la valeur ou même le gain menacé par ce risque. On la retrouve dans la commission prélevée par le banquier, dans les prix surélevés du marchand qui livre à crédit, dans les taux parfois usuraires de certains prêts."—Michel Lacombe, "Assurances," Say and Chailley's *Nouveau Dictionnaire d' Économie Politique,* vol. i, p. 101.

transferred to regular insurance companies; the former is more frequently used of the preparation to meet risks of kinds which insurance companies do not assume. While it may be impossible to avoid the use of the term insurance in referring to these forms of economic activity, it is evident that in common usage the word is ordinarily employed in a different sense. It is used to denote the transfer of risk. Any person who guarantees another against accidental loss of any kind is said to insure him. It is in this sense that the capitalist-entrepreneur insures the capital of those from whom he borrows. This use of the term insurance, however, like the preceding, fails to bring out its real significance. To apply it to all individualistic preparation for uncertain loss extends it too far in one direction; to apply it to every transfer of risk extends it too far in another. To form a complete conception of insurance, it is necessary to add to the notions of accumulation of capital and transfer of risks the idea of the combination of the risks of many individuals in a group. We should define insurance, then, as that social device for making accumulations to meet uncertain losses of capital which is carried out through the transfer of the risks of many individuals to one person or to a group of persons. Wherever there is accumulation for uncertain losses, or wherever there is a transfer of risk, there is one element of insurance; only where these are joined with the combination of risks in a group is the insurance complete.

In many respects the increase in the number of distinct risks that an individual producer carries is analogous to the combination of the risks of many individuals. Other things being equal, a ship-owner who has a hundred ships, and who carries his own insurance, is in the same economic condition as any one of a hundred ship-owners, each possessing one ship, who have combined their risks in a group through a system of insurance. The gain from the combination of risks is due solely to the increase in the number of risks in the group; and if that increase takes place through the growth of a single industry, the same advantage is obtained. It is partly because of this fact that large industrial concerns are able to carry their own insurance. With the increase in the number of distinct risks to which they are exposed, the cost of carrying the risk relatively diminishes. This gain is one of the influences that foster the growth of large industrial organizations. In the absence of all other conditions affecting their size, it would lead in the end to the concentration of each line of industry, or even of all lines, in the hands of a single organization; and in the presence of these other conditions, the size that would finally be found most advantageous would be affected by the increase in the number of risks.

It is time to point out the exact nature of the gain under consideration. It is evident that it will not be due to any reduction in the actual amount of positive loss. What the increase in the number of separate risks in the group does bring about is a reduction of the uncertainty for the group as a whole, a substitution of certain loss for uncertain loss. As was pointed out in the first chapter, the probable variation of the actual loss in any year from the average for a series of years increases only as the square root of the number of separate chances of loss included in a group. Now, as we have seen, it is through the accumulation for meeting uncertain loss that the special reward for risk-taking is obtained. Competition will not cut the accumulation for this purpose down to the average amount of loss; it leaves a margin of safety. It is evident, therefore, that anything that diminishes the degree of uncertainty reduces the cost of risk to society. As the uncertainty diminishes, the accumulation to meet the uncertain loss is brought nearer to the probable loss as estimated by the law of averages. If all the uncertainty could be annihilated, the accumulation would be limited to the exact amount of the foreseen loss, as in the case of any other fixed element in the cost of production.

The application of this principle to the institution of insurance is evident at a glance. The risk that an insurance company carries is far less than the sum of the risks of the insured,[2] and as the size of the company increases the disproportion becomes greater. It is primarily through this reduction of uncertainty that a static society would be benefited by the existence of insurance. The cost of commodities would be reduced through the diminution of that part of the expense of producing them that is involved in the necessity of paying for the assumption of risk. The

---

2 "The aggregate danger is less than the sum of the individual dangers, for the reason that it is more certain, and that uncertainty of itself is an element of danger." William Roscher, *Principles of Political Economy,* Translated by J. J. Lalor. New York, 1878, vol. ii, p. 261.

nature of this gain may be made clear by a simple illustration.

Let us assume that there are 10,000 capitalists of the same reluctance to incur risk, each owning a house valued at $5,000; that all the houses are exposed to the same danger of destruction by fire; that the average annual loss for a period of years has been 50, and the average variation 20; and that the rate of interest in safe investments is 3 per cent. If each owner makes an allowance of 3 per cent a year for the amortization fund, what annual rental will he demand for his house?

The uncertainty to which each investor is exposed is the resultant of two factors, the average loss and the probable variation. What would be the reluctance of an investor to incur the risk in the case assumed, and what reward would be necessary to overcome the reluctance, are empirical facts that we have no means of discovering. It is a conservative estimate that on account of the risk each capitalist will demand an extra one per cent on his investment. The annual rent will then be at the rate of 7 per cent, that is, $350 for each house. At the end of a decade, if the favorable and unfavorable years just offset one another, the group will have suffered a loss of 500 houses, valued at $2,500,000. This gives an average annual loss of $25 for each of the 10,000 investors. Meantime each of them has received $50 a year on account of the risk. In the group as a whole the destroyed capital has been replaced, and each investor has received a net reward of $25. The hirer of the house, who has had to pay this additional rent, is not at all concerned with the way in which the income has been distributed among the different owners. Some of these have suffered losses which the $50 a year was not enough to cover; others have escaped loss, and the entire $50 represents a net gain for them. Each consumer, in this case each house-renter, has had to pay $25 a year more than he would have had to pay if it had not been for the uncertainty.

Now let us examine the situation of the same persons after a system of insurance has been introduced. We will leave out of consideration the incidental expense of the insurance itself, and for the sake of simplicity it will be assumed that the reluctance of the insurer to assume risk is the same as that of the house-owners, and that the fact that the houses are insured has no effect upon the probability of loss. What is the uncertainty to which the insurer is exposed when he is carrying the risk of the entire group, and what reward can he obtain for assuming it?

As the average variation of the annual loss has been 20, we may assume that a minimum loss of 25 houses for the group is certain to occur each year. The insurer, then, has to face a certain loss of 25 houses a year, and a probable loss, as determined by past experience, of 25 more. For the former, the competition of other insurers will prevent him from obtaining more than enough to replace the loss. That will be $125,000 for the group, or $12.50 for each house. For the uncertain loss we will assume that he will be able to obtain a return of twice the probable amount of loss, just as the single investor did, though there are reasons why he would probably demand rather less. That will make this part of his income $250,000 for the group, or $25 for each house. Each house-owner, therefore, will have to pay the insurer $37.50 a year, and their competition with one another will prevent any one of them from obtaining more than that from the person to whom he lets the house. The entire rent will now be $337.50 a year. Each consumer saves $12.50 a year, and each capitalist is still rewarded at the same rate as before for carrying risk. If these 10,000 houses had been joined with a large number of others, so that there were, let us say, 1,000,000 in the group, a similar calculation would show that the cost of the risk to each hirer of a house would be reduced to $26.25 *per annum,* or only $1.25 more than enough to cover the actual loss in a series of years.

That this gain is in no way dependent on the combination of the risks of different investors in one group, and that it could equally well be obtained by a single concern with an increasing number of risks is manifest. It is equally manifest that it would be advantageous for a person with a large number of risks to join them with as many others of the same kind as possible. While so-called self-insurance becomes cheaper as the number of risks increases, it would never be as cheap as regular insurance if the insurance business were rightly managed. If it is cheaper for a concern to carry its own risk than to pay premiums to an insurance company, it shows either that the company considers the risk higher than the concern thinks is right, or that the insurance business is so expensively managed that the cost of the management more than offsets the gain from the increase in the number of risks. The prevalence of the custom of self-insurance against risks such as the regular insurance companies assume is a serious reflection on the management of the companies.

The effect of the principle that we are considering on the size of insurance companies is the same as that already noted in speaking of independent industrial organizations. It is a force working towards large companies. The larger an insurance company is, the cheaper it can afford to give insurance. It might be impracticable, but it would not be economically unjustifiable, to require small companies to carry higher reserves in proportion to the amount insured than large companies are compelled to carry. In the absence of conflicting influences each branch of insurance would finally be concentrated in the hands of a single company. Nor is there any reason why the process of centralization should stop here. There is the same economic advantage in combining risks of entirely different kinds, provided they are correctly estimated, as there is in combining risks of the same kind. The difficulties in the way of such general combinations are all of a practical nature. Whatever may be said on the ground of expediency for the laws passed by some of our states restricting the freedom of insurance companies in the matter of assuming different kinds of risks, economic theory affords no justification for such a policy. The more risks the cheaper the insurance, is a universal economic principle. One enormous company carrying all static risks would be the ideal organization of insurance in the static state.

The gain due to the combination of risks and to the consequent reduction of uncertainty is not the only economic benefit of insurance. There is another advantage resulting from the transfer of risk, which is of the same kind as the one previously noticed in speaking of the capitalist-entrepreneur. It is desirable for society that risks should be correctly estimated. Men differ much in their ability to judge them. The segregation of the work of estimating risks leads to a differentiation of capitalists, as a result of which those who are especially adapted to that task will be the ones who will undertake it. Moreover, their natural ability will be further developed through the experience and training of the work itself. On the other hand there are many men capable of rendering good service to society in comparatively safe industries, who are so constituted that the necessity of running any great chance of loss seriously diminishes their efficiency. The possibility of transferring the risks of their business to others for a fixed premium frees them from the paralyzing influence of uncertainty, and enables them to make the best use of their powers in other directions. The gain to society from the transfer of risks is obtained partly through the reduction in the cost of carrying the risks when they are borne by those who have the most ability to estimate them and the most confidence in their own judgments about them, and partly through the increase in the efficiency of those who are abnormally sensitive to the influence of uncertainty.

The gains of which we have been speaking are partly offset by the cost of carrying on the insurance business. This cost consists of interest on the capital and wages for the labor employed in the actual performance of the work. What that cost ought to be, if insurance companies were economically conducted, and how far the actual cost exceeds that amount, we need not stop to inquire. There is a generous margin between the price for which a large insurance company can afford to assume a risk and the price which an individual producer would demand for carrying it. That this margin is not exhausted even by the extravagant methods of management that characterize existing insurance companies is proved by the almost universal prevalence of the custom of insurance. That it is more nearly exhausted than it ought to be is proved by the persistence of the custom of self-insurance. It must not be forgotten, however, that insurance companies carry on many other forms of activity besides their special work of furnishing insurance. Investment is a prominent feature of so-called life insurance, and preventive measures of various kinds are carried out by insurers of property. Insurers of boilers have their inspectors, fire insurance companies have their patrols, burglarly insurance companies their private watchmen, and so on through the list. The part of the premium which is used in carrying out these protective measures ought not to be considered as part of the cost of insurance. It is work that would have to be done in some form by individual producers or by society, if it were not performed by the companies. The fact that the companies do it is an indication that it is accomplished more cheaply or more efficiently by them than it could be by the insured themselves. Another legitimate form of expense that ought to be recognized is the cost of securing the services of experts in appraising property and estimating risks. This work would also have to be performed in some way by individual producers if they carried their own risks. It might perhaps be accomplished more cheaply by them, but it would certainly be done more crudely and inaccurately. The gain from the accurate valuation of risks by experts more than counterbalances the necessary increase in the expense.

There is another form of loss of serious proportions which must not be left unnoticed in comparing the advantages and disadvantages of insurance. It is an essential feature of a perfect system of insurance that the occurrence of the event for whose economic consequences compensation is guaranteed shall never be a source of gain to the insured. In an ideally complete system the payment by the insurance company will just equal the loss of the insured. Now it is a matter of common observation that insurance is often obtained in excess of the actual value of the property insured. As a consequence there is considerable wilful destruction of property for the purpose of obtaining the insurance. Moreover, it is doubtful whether it is practically desirable that the amount of the insurance equal the full value of the property, since no incentive would be left to the insured to guard against the destruction of his property. Over-insurance leads to fraud, full insurance to carelessness, and even partial insurance to some diminution of watchfulness. Whatever increase may occur in the amount of positive loss either through fraud or through carelessness must be deducted from the diminution in negative loss in estimating the net gain which insurance brings to society.

The economic significance of insurance in a static state is connected with its influence in reducing the burden which the existence of risk imposes on society. So far as the degree of risk is lowered, and the reluctance to assume it is diminished, so far is society benefited by the institution of insurance. How great the gain is, even under existing imperfect conditions, it is impossible to estimate, since it is difficult to conceive how the large enterprises of the present day could be carried on without the possibility of transferring to insurance companies many of the risks involved in them. It could certainly be done only on a much larger margin of safety than is now considered necessary.

The essential features of economic insurance as we have defined it are the accumulation of capital to meet uncertain losses, and the transfer and combination of risks. Many other conceptions of insurance have been held by various writers on the subject. Some originated in an over-emphasis of a comparatively unimportant phase of the institution, others in a wrong interpretation of some feature of it. As an example of the former kind may be mentioned the conception of those writers who find the significance of insurance in the diffusion of positive losses over a large group of persons.[3] That the insured in the long run pay all the losses is undoubtedly true, but the distribution of the losses is only an indirect result of the insurance; it is neither the purpose of it nor the immediate consequence. The purpose of securing insurance is to avoid uncertainty. The insured buys security by the payment of a fixed premium, and after he has bought it his condition is not affected by the number of losses which the insurer may have to make good. If the number of losses increases, the premium rate may be raised; but in all cases of complete insurance the cost of it is a definite element in the expense of production, the amount of which is fixed before the occurrence of the losses. Only in the case of mutual assessment companies is there a direct distribution of losses over a group. A member of such a company is not in the same economic situation as one insured for a fixed premium. He has not transferred his risk and purchased security; he has exchanged one risk for another, usually a small chance of a large loss for a larger chance of a smaller loss. Where there is a mere diffusion of loss there remains some degree of uncertainty as to the amount of loss that each member of the group will suffer;

3 "Considerée dans son principe même, l'assurance est une association qui a pour objet de répartir entre tous ses membres les pertes occasionnées à quelques-uns d'entre eux par certains événements fortuits, de telle sorte que chaque membre supporte sa part de l'indemnité due aux victimes du sinistre." —Ch. Dumaine, "Assurances," Say's Dictionnaire des Finances, vol. i, p. 220.

"Versicherung im wirthschaftlichen Sinne ist diejenige wirthschaftliche Einrichtung, welche die nachtheiligen Folgen (zukünftigen) einzelner, für den Betroffenen zufälliger, daher auch im einzelnen Falle ihres Eintretens unvorhergesehener Ereignisse für das Vermögen einer Person dadurch beseitigt oder wenigstens vermindert dass sie dieselben auf eine Reihe von Fällen vertheilt, in denen die gleiche Gefahr droht, aber nicht wirklich eintritt."—Adolph Wagner, "Versicherungswesen," Schönberg's Handbuch, 4te Auf, 2 Band 2, s. 359.

where there is complete insurance the insurer has taken upon himself the entire chance of loss, so far as concerns the risks covered by the insurance. To define insurance, then, as the distribution of losses is to make too prominent an indirect and comparatively unimportant result of it, and to leave entirely out of the definition the elements in which its economic significance really lies.

The other erroneous conception of insurance to which reference has been made is even more indefensible than the one just noticed. Instead of arising from an over-emphasis of a comparatively unimportant feature of the institution, it is based on an essentially false idea of its nature. Because each insurance contract considered by itself is a contingent contract, and because the event upon which the payment by the insurer to the insured depends is uncertain, many writers have regarded insurance as a form of gambling.[4] But the resemblance is in reality of the most superficial kind. It is not difficult to discover the mark of distinction between the two transactions. Insurance involves the transfer of an existing risk from one person to another; gambling involves the creation of a new risk to which neither party to the transaction was exposed before the contract, and to which they are both exposed after it. If a man insures his factory, he frees himself from uncertainty, and the other party to the contract assumes it; if he makes a wager with another, his own uncertainty and that of the other person are both increased at the same time. Undoubtedly in the past many transactions which wore the virtuous guise of insurance were no better than gambling contracts. If a person takes out a policy on property in which he has no insurable interest, he

4 "Let us now contrast the workings of insurance. In this case also the contract is a wager. A house-owner pays an insurance company fifty dollars, in return for which he is to receive five thousand dollars in case his house burns down within a specified time; just as he might pay a bookmaker fifty dollars and receive five thousand in case a specified horse wins a race."—Arthur T. Hadley, Economics, p. 99.

"Le contrat aléatoire est une convention réciproque dont les effêts, quant aux avantages et aux pertes soit pour toutes les parties, soit pour l'une ou plusieurs d'entre elles, dépendent d'un événement incertain. Telles sont le contrat d'assurance, . . . le jeu et le pari, . . ."—Code civil français, Art. 1984. Quoted in Charles Berdez, Les Bases de l'Assurance Privée, p. 36, note.

"Wenn also der unorganisierte Spiel des Schicksals den Menschen in Gefahr bringt, so begreifen wir, dass das Mittel, welches er ihm entgegensetzt, ein organisiertes Glückspiel sein wird. Er erreicht dadurch die Wirkung, dass er zur selben Zeit, wo er von eineme Verlust betroffen wird, durch das Glückspiel einen Gewinn erhält, der gerade den Schaden deckt."—R. Schlink, Die Natur der Versicherung, Würzburg, 1887, s. 13.

virtually makes a wager with the insurance company that the property will be destroyed. Such contracts are clearly against public policy, and legislation has done much to limit their number. The courts on the other hand have frequently given a liberal construction to the phrase "insurable interest," and many contracts of doubtful legitimacy are still tolerated. A legitimate insurance contract, however, may always be distinguished from a gambling contract by the principle pointed out. Insurance is the transfer of risk, gambling the creation of risk.

After a system of insurance against any class of risks has been established, an entrepreneur has a choice between three methods of meeting such a risk in an industry that he has decided to enter. He may adopt preventive measures, he may obtain insurance, or he may carry the risk and pay a higher price for the capital he borrows. His selection among these different modes of conduct will depend upon their relative cost. Expenditure for any one of them is to him an item in the cost of production, and he will naturally adopt the one that is cheapest. As a matter of fact, in nearly all cases it is necessary to combine the three methods. Preventive measures are adopted by which the total amount of risk is somewhat reduced; a part of the remaining risk is transferred to insurance companies; the rest is borne by the capital in the industry. The amount of the expenditure for each of these purposes is determined according to the principles already established. The payment for the capital exposed to risk contains an element of reward for risk-taking, which is large in proportion to the degree of risk; the payment for insurance contains a relatively smaller element of the same kind; the payment for prevention contains none at all.

The entire sum paid by the insured to the insurance company is called the insurance premium. As the companies carry on many forms of activity which are not an essential part of their business of furnishing insurance, and the expense of which is paid out of the premiums they receive, the cost of the insurance itself is less than the amount of the premium. In a strict economic sense the insurance premium includes only that part of the payment to the company that would have to be made to induce it to assume the risk. Expenditures for preventive measures, whether made directly by the entrepreneur himself, or first incurred by the insurance company and then recovered from the insured, are no part of the cost of insurance. This distinction, however, is not observed by all writers.[5] Because the entrepreneur has a choice between prevention and insurance, it seems to be inferred that the two forms of expenditure are essentially alike. It is evident, however, that if all expenditures for the purpose of preventing accidental loss are to be regarded as insurance premiums, a very considerable part of the cost of production must come under that head. Such an extension of the term insurance utterly destroys its economic significance. Nor is the situation much improved by limiting its application to the expenditures for those preventive measures that make it possible to obtain insurance from organized companies at a lower rate. The distinction does not depend on any such accidental circumstance as that. It goes back to the fundamental difference between the methods by which the amounts of the two kinds of payments are determined. One includes an element of reward for risk-taking, which in the case of insurance goes to the insurer, whose capital is bearing the risk; the other is determined by the direct cost of introducing the preventive measure, whether the work is done by the entrepreneur himself or by the company. Prevention and insurance are complementary methods of preparing to meet uncertain losses; only confusion can result from the attempt to make them identical.

Not only do insurance companies carry on many forms of activity that are no part of their peculiar functions as insurers, but not all their activity as insurers has any direct bearing on the productivity of capital. The insurance of consumption goods is almost as common as the insurance of capital goods. It would not be difficult, in the light of the principles already discussed, to discover the laws that determine the adoption of insurance by the owners of consumption goods, or the nature of the social service that such insurance renders. A study of that sort would not be without interest, but it is outside the range of our

[5] See, for example, Alfred Marshall, *Principles of Economics*, vol. i, p. 469, note. "Again, certain insurance companies in America take risks against fire in factories at very much less than the ordinary rates, on condition that some prescribed precautions are taken, such as providing automatic sprinklers, and making the walls and floors solid. The expense incurred in these arrangements is really an insurance premium. . . ."

investigation. We are concerned only with the insurance of capital, that is, with insurance as a method of lowering the cost of producing commodities.

Insurance is primarily a method of making accumulations to meet uncertain losses. Attention has already been called to the gain that accrues to society through the reduction in the amount of such accumulations which insurance brings about. There are one or two other points in connection with this aspect of the institution that deserve consideration. Capital alone can insure capital. The guarantee of security by one who had no means of making good the losses that occurred would be a fruitless proceeding. The amount of capital necessary to give security evidently depends on the amount of risk that the capital assumes. As the number of risks carried by an insurance company increases, the amount of its accumulations also must increase. Stock companies start with a certain amount of capital contributed by the members of the company, and make additional accumulations out of the contributions of the insured. Mutual companies, if they are to perform their functions perfectly, must also make accumulations of the same kind, but these funds are all contributed by the insured themselves, who virtually constitute the company. From the point of view of economic theory the difference between the two kinds of companies is of no significance. One form of insurance is not necessarily any cheaper than the other. If the entire business of insurance were on a strictly competitive basis, and if the accumulations of the companies were in all cases limited to the amounts necessary to give security, it would be a matter of no importance by whom the funds were contributed. Capital is invested in the business of insurance for the same purpose that any other investment is made—in order to obtain a reward. If the insuring fund of the mutual companies is made up out of the current contributions of the insured, the owners of the capital thus invested will require in some form the same return on their capital that they could obtain in any other investment with the same degree of risk. The members of the mutual company are carrying on the business of insurance with a part of their capital, which acts as a guarantee fund for the capital that they have invested in more hazardous enterprises. The gain accrues to the insured as insurers instead of accruing to the members of a stock company. As there is no reason why the accumulations of mutual companies should be any less than the accumulations of stock companies, of which the capital stock forms a part, there is no reason why the return to the capital thus invested should be any less in the former than in the latter. Whatever gain can be secured under competitive conditions by insuring in a mutual company rather than in a stock company is due to the fact that the insured themselves have invested capital in the insurance business.

How large the accumulations of insurance companies ought to be in proportion to the risks they carry, can be determined only by experience. The prime requisite of such an institution is security. Therefore the accumulations must be large enough to cover the probable losses, with a margin of safety for unexpectedly large ones. It is safe to say, however, that the accumulations of many companies are in excess of the amount thus determined. I do not refer here to the accumulations made by life insurance companies, which combine entirely different functions with that of insurance, and a large part of whose funds represent simply investments of capital by the insured. Nor do I include that part of the funds of insurance companies which is used for other purposes than insurance, such as the expenditures for preventive measures. That part of their accumulations which is strictly an insurance fund is often larger than it needs to be. The possibility of making such unnecessarily large accumulations is due to imperfect competition, which does not force the cost of insurance down to the competitive level. If, however, it were necessary for these funds to lie idle in the vaults of the company, it is evident that there would be no motive for making accumulations larger than the conditions of the business demanded. Any excess would be distributed as dividends among the stockholders of the company, or, in a mutual company, would result in an immediate lowering of the insurance premium. That this distribution of the entire surplus does not take place is explained by the fact that capital which is insuring the other capital is not prevented on that ground from participating in other forms of industrial activity. We have already seen in the case of the capitalist-entrepreneur that while his own capital acts as a guarantee fund for the capital that he borrows, it at the same time performs its part in the direct productive activity of the industry in which it is invested. The fulfilment of the insurance contract does not require the creation of new capital; it requires merely the transfer of the ownership of existing capital. Therefore the accumulated funds of insurance companies, even that part of them which is economically necessary, instead of remaining otherwise unproductive, are invested in such ways that they earn an income for the company. Of course there are certain restrictions as to the forms in which such investments should be made. For practical reasons it is desirable that the funds should be invested where there is the least danger of loss, and where the difficulty of realizing on the investments is at a minimum. But the important point is that capital which is insuring other capital may at the same time be directly employed in the production of wealth. The unnecessarily large surpluses of insurance companies are allowed to accumulate, not for the sake of the reward they can obtain in the insurance business, but for the sake of the interest paid for their use by those to whom they are lent.

It is evident that the possibility of using productively the reserve funds of insurance companies reduces the cost of insurance. Under competitive conditions the return that capital invested in the insurance business can secure will be fixed. In the long run it will consist of pure interest plus the reward for carrying the risk to which it is exposed. All other income that the companies receive will operate to reduce the payments of the insured. If it were necessary for reserve funds to remain unproductive, the income that they now earn would have to be obtained from the insured in the form of higher premiums.

One question in this connection remains to be answered. In what sense is the employment of capital to insure other capital a productive function? The difficulty in answering this question is due to two circumstances. On the one hand, capital which is insuring other capital may at the same time be productively employed in other ways and create the same amount of physical product as any other capital so employed. On the other hand, the reward which capital obtains for insuring other capital is entirely created by the capital that is insured. It is evident, therefore, that insuring capital, as such, is not directly creating physical product. Its service is to create a condition which increases the productivity of the capital that is insured. In return for this service a part of the product of the insured capital is handed over to the insurer. But this is not to deny the productivity of the insuring capital. In an economic sense the product of a unit of capital is the part of the total product whose creation is due to the presence of that particular unit. If, then, the insuring capital, by virtue of its service in guaranteeing safety, increases the total product of the insured capital, the additional part must be attributed to the insuring capital as its product. If there were a monopoly of the privilege of granting insurance, the entire increase in product might be appropriated by the insurers. Perfect competition, on the other hand, would bring about an influx of capital into the insuring business which in the end would reduce the total return to capital in it to the same proportions as the return to capital in any other industry involving the same degree of risk. The remainder of the economic gain due to the existence of the institution of insurance would then accrue chiefly to the consumers of the commodities created in the industries in which the insured capital is employed. There is no fundamental difference in kind between the reward for risk-taking which accrues to capital employed directly in a hazardous enterprise and the reward which insuring capital obtains for the risk it assumes. In both cases there is an increased productivity of industry on account of the assumption of the risk, and in both cases the capital exposed to risk obtains a part of the increased product as its special reward. In both cases, moreover, the amount of the extra reward which capital can obtain by assuming risk is fixed by the sacrifice of the most reluctant investor whose capital is needed to meet the demands of society. The only difference between the two kinds of income is the comparatively unimportant one that in the former case the extra product is created directly by the capital that receives it, while in the latter case it is created by other capital and handed over to the insuring capital as a reward for creating the conditions which make possible the increased productivity of the capital which is insured.

The statement is sometimes made that all insurance is mutual insurance.[6] It is evident from a consideration of the facts already established that this is only partially true. All insurance is mutual in the sense that all the losses are in the long run paid by the insured. Obviously an insurance company could not long survive if it systematically made good the losses of the insured out of its own capital. To the company the payment of losses is an element in the cost of carrying on its business, and in the long run consumers necessarily pay all the expenses of production. This mutual aspect of insurance, however, does not bring out its fundamental significance. This lies in the reduction of the cost of producing commodities through the relief of producers from the disagreeable feelings aroused by uncertainty, and the substitution of security for insecurity. The burden of insecurity which would rest upon individual producers in the absence of a system of insurance is in no way borne by the insured as a body after insurance has been introduced. A large part of it is entirely annihilated, and the remainder rests upon the insurers whose capital has assumed the risks of the insured. Even in the case of so-called mutual companies, while the surviving uncertainty is still borne by the members of the company, the real significance of the institution does not lie in this fact, but in the reduction of the uncertainty as a result of the insurance. The over-emphasis of its importance in causing a diffusion of loss is due to an imperfect analysis of its economic effects.

Insurance is evidently far from being a gratuitous gift to society. The component parts of its cost are the wages of the labor employed in the insurance business, interest on the capital invested in it, and any increase in the amount of positive loss through fraud or carelessness, which the existence of insurance induces. This cost first falls upon the entrepreneurs who choose to insure their capital rather than to pay capitalists a higher price on account of risk. To the entrepreneurs, therefore, it is a part of the cost of production; it will be embodied in the price of the commodities, and will thus be shifted to the shoulders of consumers. It is in the end the consuming public that pays the entire expense of insurance. This does not by any means imply that the

6 See, for example, H. C. Emery, "The Place of the Speculator in the Theory of Distribution," *Publications of the American Economic Association*, 3d Series, vol. i, no. 1, p. 105.

condition of consumers is not benefited by the existence of insurance. The comparison lies, not between the cost of insurance and no cost, but between the cost of insurance and the cost of risk without insurance. The gain to the consumer comes through the reduction in the price of commodities, and the amount of the reduction is determined by the difference between the interest which the entrepreneur would have to pay for capital exposed to the entire risk of the industry on the one hand, and the lower interest on the capital when it is insured, plus the cost of the insurance itself on the other hand.

There has been a singular lack of unanimity among writers on political economy with regard to the division of economic theory in which the treatment of insurance ought to be placed. Some have considered it in connection with production, others have regarded it as a phenomenon of consumption, while still others have found it inexpedient to bring it under any of the recognized divisions, and have put it at the end of their works along with other subjects of a more or less dubious economic character. There seems to be little occasion for such uncertainty. If the old divisions of production, distribution, exchange and consumption are to be maintained, there is no doubt that the proper place for the discussion of insurance, at least so far as insurance of capital is concerned, is in the department of production. With regard to the insurance of consumption goods the case may not seem so plain at first sight, since there is not the same direct relation between such insurance and the productivity of industry. Nevertheless, it undoubtedly belongs in the division of production. It belongs there, not because it affects the productivity of other capital, but because the creation of security is in itself a form of production. If the owners of consumption goods are willing to pay a price for the sake of having them insured, it is evident that they are obtaining something in exchange which is of more value to them than the money with which they part. What they obtain is security, and whether or not it seems best to consider such security as a consumption good, or as any form of wealth, it cannot be questioned that the capital and labor engaged in creating it are serving mankind in the same way as that employed in the creation of any commodity for which consumers are willing to pay.

The conclusions reached in the present chapter are in part as follows: Complete insurance, in the economic sense, is the accumulation of funds for uncertain losses and the combination of the risks of individuals in a group. The advantage of such an institution in a static society would be the result of its influence in reducing the burden of risk. To call all insurance mutual, or to define it as the distribution of losses, is to put the emphasis on a comparatively unimportant aspect of it; to call it gambling is to confuse forms of activity fundamentally different both in their purpose and in their consequences. Capital employed in insuring other capital is productive, and the reward it receives is a part of its product. Capital employed in insuring consumption goods is creating something for which the owners of the goods are willing to pay. It, therefore, is also productive. The treatment of insurance naturally belongs in the division of economic theory that deals with the phenomena of the production of wealth.

CHAPTER VIII

CONCLUSION

Before attempting to give a summary of the static theory of risk and insurance developed in previous chapters, it may be worth while to consider briefly one or two special phases of the influence of risk in a dynamic society. No attempt will be made to work out a complete dynamic theory. Static laws are comparatively easy to discover, since the economic forces at work in a static society are by hypothesis few and simple. In a dynamic society the conditions are very different. Dynamic changes are continually introducing disturbances into the economic system. The new forces modify the action of the static forces, sometimes reinforcing them and sometimes opposing them, and the simplicity of the static state is replaced by the apparent irregularity and confusion of the existing industrial world. That this irregularity is only apparent, and that with the progress of economic science general principles will be discovered by which the movements of a dynamic society can be classified and traced to their sources, is undoubtedly true. It is in this field that the most difficult and most important work of economic theory remains to be done. It will naturally be divided into two parts. One will deal with the laws governing the dynamic changes themselves, and the other will trace the working of the laws of the static state under dynamic conditions. It is in the second of these divisions that the following brief discussions would fall. The most that will be attempted is to point out the bearing of the static laws of risk already discovered on certain dynamic problems. We shall take up only these three questions: the influence of risk upon the accumulation of capital, the relation of the entrepreneur to developmental risks and the economic character of the service of the speculator as insurer.

Risk retards the rate of accumulation of capital. Every increase in the amount of capital, other things being equal, diminishes the productivity and reward of each unit of it. On the other hand, every additional unit of capital saved, other things being equal, involves an increased sacrifice on the part of the person saving it. Saving is carried by each individual to the point when the sacrifice and the reward offset each other, and then it ceases. Now the necessity of exposing capital to risk increases the sacrifice involved in saving. Saving ceases while the marginal productivity of capital is still high enough to reward the risk-taking as well as the abstinence. If the degree of risk were uniform in all investments, it is evident that the extent of the influence in this direction would depend entirely upon this uniform degree of risk. With unequal degrees of risk, the relation between the risk and the accumulation of capital is not quite so simple. The effect of the risk is determined immediately by the relation between the risk and the reward in safe investments. But the rate of interest here is itself affected by the risk in other investments. We have seen how the requirement by capitalists of an abnormally high reward in hazardous industries reduces the return in safe industries below the normal level. When the risk in different investments is unequal, therefore, its influence in retarding accumulation is much greater than would be inferred from the degree of risk in those which are safest. In order to determine what that influence is, it would be necessary to calculate some sort of an average of the risks in all investments. It is possible that this might be taken at a point where greater and smaller risks are so balanced that the productivity of capital is not affected by the inequality in the degrees of risk. The reward necessary to overcome the reluctance to incur this average degree of risk determines the margin of saving.

As risk retards the accumulation of capital, anything that reduces the degree of risk or the reluctance to assume it promotes accumulation. Insurance in a dynamic society may be regarded as a method of fostering the growth of capital. The gain in question is not at all the one on which enthusiastic life insurance agents lay so much stress. Whatever may be the advantage of so-called life and endowment insurance as forms of investment, furnishing opportunity for investment is no part of the insuring function.

The advantage to which we refer is of a more fundamental character. It is due to the influence of insurance in extending the range of safe investments. There are large amounts of capital, such as trust funds, savings-bank deposits, and even the reserves of the insurance companies themselves, in the investment of which safety is the prime consideration. This fact tends to reduce the rate of interest in safe investments to a very low point. Every increase in the opportunity for making such investments has an influence in retarding the fall of the rate of interest in them, and so in pushing further out the point of equilibrium between the sacrifice and the reward of saving.

One other point in connection with the influence of risk on the accumulation of capital deserves to be noticed. Just as the sacrifice of abstinence diminishes, other things being equal, as a man's income increases, so the sacrifice of risk-taking becomes less as his capital becomes greater. The result is a tendency towards a more and more unequal distribution of capital. The sacrifice of a laboring man in saving a hundred dollars from his year's income is apt to be very great. There is, therefore, need of a large reward to make him willing to undergo the sacrifice. And just because it costs so much to accumulate the capital, he feels great reluctance to expose it to the chance of loss. Safety is to him a matter of the first importance. In the use which he makes of his capital, therefore, he is confined to the least hazardous investments; and in these investments the rate of interest is near the minimum. Those who need the largest reward to make them willing to save are the ones who can obtain only the smallest reward on account of their unwillingness to incur risk.[1] By far the larger part of the savings of society come out of the incomes of large capitalists and entrepreneurs; the contributions of laborers and small capitalists are comparatively insignificant. Now the increase of capital is in itself almost an unmixed good. Moreover, there are certain advantages in its unequal distribution. The total saving of society is thereby increased, and the existing capital is more productively employed. The growth of large fortunes in recent years has done much to extend the margin of industry into the territory of hazardous enterprises. Even the small capitalists are indirectly benefited thereby,

[1] In considering the influence of the rate of interest on accumulation some allowance ought undoubtedly to be made for the tendency of a fall in the rate of interest to induce larger savings on the part of those who are chiefly concerned to assure to themselves or their families a certain fixed income.

through the drawing off of capital from safe investments and the retardation in the fall of the rate of interest in them. But it is possible to pay too high a price for the gain thus realized. The accumulation of capital is not an end in itself, nor is its distribution a matter of no importance. Clearly every device that will promote saving on the part of the laboring class is to be welcomed; and it can hardly be doubted that a less unequal distribution of capital, even though it involved some falling off in the productivity of industry as a whole, would increase the sum total of human welfare. The influence of insurance, so far as it widens the range of safe investments and thus promotes saving on the part of people of small resources, has a tendency to reduce the inequalities in the distribution of wealth.

The influence of private ownership of land in promoting saving is also worthy of note. I do not refer to the well known fact that the desire of the average man to own a piece of ground stimulates his productive activity. It is the influence of the security of the investment to which I wish to call attention. In spite of local fluctuations in value as population shifts from place to place, investments in land under normal conditions have always been regarded as exceptionally secure. A very considerable part of the savings of small capitalists has for this reason been placed in this form of investment, either directly or through the medium of savings-banks and building and loan associations. The withdrawal of land from private ownership would reduce the area of safe investments to such a degree as to cause a serious fall in the rate of interest in them. Whatever may be said on other grounds for or against private ownership of land, it cannot be questioned that on account of the wide opportunity for safe investment which it affords it has a great influence in promoting saving by persons of small means.

From the same point of view, no greater service could be rendered society than that which would result from the introduction of a method of giving security to the bonds of large industrial corporations. Something is already accomplished in this direction through the custom of underwriting which has been growing in recent years. A large banking concern undertakes to float a loan for a corporation, and to give to the bonds the backing of its own reputation, on condition that the directors of the corporation agree to observe certain principles in the management of their property. The object of this stipulation is to prevent unwise action on the part of the directors, such as would tend to injure the earning capacity of the property and impair the security of the bonds. Obviously such action is limited both in its range and in its efficiency. The invention of a system of guarantee and control which would give to the bonds of all established corporations the security which now attaches only to government bonds would enormously increase the opportunity for safe investment, would raise the rate of interest in such investments well above its present level, and would thus encourage saving by those to whom the disutility of insecurity is very great.

One of the greatest services which the entrepreneur renders society is the result of his activity in opening up new avenues for the employment of capital. The growth of capital is a characteristic feature of a progressive society, and with that growth comes the necessity of finding new methods of employing it, if the rate of interest is to be kept from falling rapidly. The discovery of new methods of employing capital has the same sort of influence on the rate of interest and the incentive to save as the extension of the range of safe investments. Of the different ways in which new capital may be employed, and the different degrees of risk involved in them, enough has already been said. A few points remain to be noticed about the relation of the entrepreneur to this kind of risk.

The incentive to activity by which an entrepreneur is led is the hope of realizing a profit. Now the origin of profit is always in change. It is of the nature of entrepreneurs, therefore, to be continually experimenting with new methods, new machinery and new products. There are very unequal degrees of risk involved in these experiments. In some cases it is practically certain from the moment the new idea is conceived that the application of it will lead to the appearance of a large profit; in others the outcome is a matter of a great deal of uncertainty. As we have already seen, there is no constant relation between the degree of uncertainty and the amount of profit. Still it is evident that of two equally uncertain experiments the one would first be tried in which the profit would be larger in case of success; and that of two experiments holding out hope of equal profit, the less uncertain one would be first undertaken. This seems to indicate some sort of relationship between risk and profit. What is it, however, that limits the action of entrepreneurs in this way?

So far as the experiment involves danger to existing capital, their choice may be due to their unwillingness to expose their own capital to danger, or to the difficulty of obtaining capital from others for such a purpose. If entrepreneurs were able to obtain gratuitously all the capital they wished, there would be no such limitation to their unwillingness to incur risk. It would still be true, however, that a certain profit would have more attraction than an uncertain one of the same size. Any one naturally prefers a certain gain to an uncertain one. Moreover, an entrepreneur has to devote time and labor to the manage- ment of his business, and must have a reasonable assurance of receiving at least as large a return from it as he could obtain by selling his services to others. Finally, the reputation for sound judgment and efficient management, which continued success gives, is of value to him, since it enables him to secure capital at a lower rate. This reputation, however, is a part of his equip- ment as a laborer, and would increase his wages if he sold his services to others. The extra reward that he obtains for risking it is a part of his wages of management and not a part of pure profit. In our discussion all consideration of that part of the entrepre- neur's income which is wages of management and which accrues to him as laborer and not as entrepreneur is excluded.

As there is a limited number of entrepreneurs, there must be a limit to the range of their activity. As a certain gain is more attractive than an uncertain gain, entrepreneurs will naturally first select those experiments in which the probability of success is great. To induce one of them to undertake a more uncertain experiment when a less uncertain one is open to him, the profit in the former, if it succeeds, must be greater than the profit in the latter. To this extent there will be a relation between the chance of obtaining a profit by undertaking an industrial experi- ment and the probable amount of the profit. It is evident, how- ever, that this extra profit is not the reward for bearing risk. Under the conditions assumed, the entrepreneur is exposed to no risk of loss in either undertaking. The amount of profit to be obtained in the more hazardous experiment is in no part due to the risk. It is determined by other conditions with which the risk has nothing to do. Although the entrepreneur obtains a larger profit by undertaking a more hazardous experiment, he does not obtain it because the experiment is more hazardous. If the only opportunity open to him were one in which the chance of success was slight and the profit in case of success not large, he would have no hesitation about undertaking the experiment, provided he risked no capital of his own and his wages of management were assured him. While, therefore, in their selection of industrial experiments entrepreneurs are naturally led to undertake first those in which there is the greatest reward in proportion to the uncertainty of success, and while in consequence there is a relation between uncertainty and profit in this class of undertakings, the action of the entrepreneur in entering upon the experiment cannot be called the assumption of risk, and the large profit is not to be confounded with the reward for risk-taking. The person who furnishes the capital, and stands to lose it if the experiment fails, bears all the risk of the undertaking. The choice of a certain profit rather than an uncertain one by the entrepreneur is the same sort of an act as the choice of a large profit rather than a small one.

On account of technical limitations the activity of insurance companies has been for the most part confined to the assumption of risks in which the existence or the possession of property was involved. They have made few attempts to insure goods of any kind against loss of value. Many commodities are liable to great fluctuations in value, and in some cases these fluctuations have serious consequences for the welfare of society. Agricultural products are commodities of this kind. That the fluctuations of their value are great is due to imperfect control of the supply by those who produce them and to the inelastic nature of the demand for them; that these fluctuations seriously affect the welfare of society is due partly to the fact that they constitute an important part of the consumption of the masses of the people, and partly to the fact that the efficient distribution of the supply requires temporary accumulations of large stocks of the goods in the hands of manufacturers and dealers. The former fact makes it difficult for people with small incomes to apportion their expenditures over a series of years to the best advantage. Excessive consumption in times of low prices is followed by too great a contraction of consumption in times of scarcity. The total utility of the commodities consumed is thereby diminished. The second fact tends to increase the price of the commodities in times of abundance and scarcity alike, since the great uncertainty incurred by investing capital in large stocks of the goods, for purposes either of manufacture or of sale, restricts the flow of capital into such investments to amounts which yield a large reward.

It is in reducing the cost of this special kind of risk that speculators serve society as insurers. By a system of transfer of risks, which will be considered in a moment, they take upon themselves the chance of gain or loss through fluctuations in the value of certain commodities in the hands of manufacturers and dealers. That this is no part of the purpose of the speculators is undoubtedly true. Their immediate object is to make money through fluctuations of prices. We need not stop to consider the general phenomena of speculation nor its influence upon society.[2] We are concerned only with that part of the activity of speculators which serves indirectly to reduce the cost of uncertainty. The way in which this service is rendered may be made clear by a concrete illustration.

A miller who buys large quantities of wheat to grind into flour is exposed to a chance of gain or loss through a change in the market price of the grain. If the price of wheat varies, the price of flour will probably vary with it. This uncertainty about the movement of prices is a disturbing factor in the miller's calculations. He frees himself from it by a transaction on the wheat market. At the same time that he buys a quantity of wheat for his mill, he sells the same amount to a speculator for future delivery. When he sells his flour he delivers the wheat. If the prices

2 See H. C. Emery, *Speculation on the Stock and Produce Exchanges of the United States*, 1896, for an account of the activities of speculators and the mechanism of stock exchanges. See also "The Place of the Speculator in the Theory of Distribution," by the same author, *Publications of the American Economic Association*, Third Series, 1, 1900, pp. 103-114, for a discussion of the question suggested by the title of the article. The illustration of the service of the speculator, given in the text, is condensed from this article.

of wheat and flour have fallen, his loss on the flour is made good by his gain on the wheat; and, on the other hand, if prices have risen, the extra gain that he realizes from the sale of the flour is used in settling his contract with the speculator. In either case he is left with the legitimate profits of his business, unaffected by any changes in the price of wheat.[3]

It is evident that for the miller this transaction is a form of insurance. By means of it he purchases security from certain dangers to which he would otherwise be exposed. Its nature is somewhat concealed by the peculiar form of the premium which the miller pays. Instead of paying a fixed amount, he surrenders to the speculator the chance of gain at the same time that he transfers to him the chance of loss. This fact, however, does not alter the real character of the transaction. It is evident that in the long run the speculators obtain the advantage, as otherwise they would not continue to render the service. Whether on account of their better information as to the condition of the market, or their greater shrewdness in anticipating future movements of prices, their contracts are made on such terms as to yield them a reward. This gain is virtually the insurance premium.

The benefit which society derives from this transaction is of the same kind as that which regular insurance companies confer. The diminution of the uncertainty to which the miller is exposed makes him willing to carry on his business on a much smaller margin than he would otherwise require. He no longer demands a large extra reward for carrying risk. How this increases the productivity of capital and causes a gain for the consumer of flour through a fall in its price, can be seen at once in the light of the principles already established.

Professor Emery raises a question as to the economic character of the service which speculators render and the category of distribution in which his income belongs. He finds it difficult to discover in the insuring activity of the speculator any recognized productive function. Thus we read: "Speculative risks stand in a way outside the *process* of production and speculative gains

---

[3] By this transaction the miller does not wholly free himself from "speculative" risk. There is a possibility of an independent change in the price of flour during the period of grinding. This risk the miller himself still carries.

constitute, not a coördinate share with wages, interest and profits, but rather such claims to the product as are represented in all property rights." Again we read: "Speculation does not directly produce wealth, but there is a real increase or decrease in the value of property due to outside causes, and this gain or loss in value is shared by speculators."

Now the appropriation by speculators of gain which accrues to property that they themselves own does not require any explanation. The possibility of such chance gains is an incident of the institution of private property. Evidently this is not what Professor Emery has in mind. It must be the appropriation by speculators of a part of the gain that accrues to the property of others that he is considering. If the owners of the property are willing to make over this gain to the speculators, the reason must be that the latter are rendering some economic service for which the former are willing to pay. Otherwise the whole affair is reduced to the plane of a gambling transaction and has no place in economic theory. The only economic claim that any one has to a share of the social product is based on the fact that he has helped to create the product. That speculators, so far as they act as insurers, use their capital and labor in a way that increases their productivity, Professor Emery himself recognizes in many places. We read, for example, "This does not mean that the speculative market is not an aid to production. It is difficult to see how a great world trade in such staples as grain and cotton would be possible without it." We are told more specifically that "Under the old method (before speculation was introduced) the trader had to allow a margin of five or ten cents a bushel on wheat to cover a possible fall in value. Today traders will carry wheat on a margin of a fraction of a cent, and the allowance for risk is practically nothing." In view of these facts and many others of a similar character which Professor Emery cites, it is not easy to understand why he is unwilling to acknowledge the productivity of the activity of the speculator. If traders carry wheat on a smaller margin, it means that less capital is needed to perform a given amount of work. In other words, the capital is more productive than it was before. This surely justifies us in calling the activity of the speculator productive. Speculation, so far as it is insurance, is a phenomenon of the

production of wealth. Distribution through this kind of speculation is a direct result of productive service.[4]

Speculation, from the point of view from which we have been
considering it, is an institution which society has created for the
purpose of obtaining security against a special class of risks. Perhaps it would be more accurate to say that the institution has
been created for other ends, some good and some bad, and has
been utilized by society for this purpose. Insurance is something
of a by-product. That other operations of speculators, which are
of very doubtful service to society, have to be set over against their
activity as insurers cannot be denied. The evils of speculation are
many and gross. It may well be hoped that in the course of time
a different method of reducing the burden of this kind of risk
may be evolved, which shall be as efficient as speculation and free
from many of its attendant evils.

The central principle of the static theory of risk, so far as it
deals with risks to capital, may be stated in a single sentence. In
the approximate static state, capital will be so apportioned under
the influence of risk that the productivity and reward of the different units, in the absence of other disturbing influences, will
vary directly as the risk to which, in the judgment of its owner, it
is exposed. The economic cost of risk in such a society would be
due to inequalities in the degree of risk in different investments.
This would prevent the perfect static apportionment of capital.
The loss of productivity on account of the uneconomic apportionment of capital is the measure of the cost of risk in a static society.

As long as man's knowledge remains imperfect, accidental destruction of capital will be an incident of the production of
wealth. The amount of such loss is far greater in some industries
than in others. If society wishes to enjoy the product of a hazard-

---

[4] Space is lacking for a consideration of the difficulties raised by Professor
Emery as to the economic identity of the speculator. There seems to be a
confusion between personal and functional distribution in his discussion. The
speculator could not secure the miller from loss unless he possessed the requisite amount of capital; he must therefore be a capitalist. A part of his income
is interest, and this is high on account of the hazardous nature of the business.
His occupation calls for the expenditure of much physical and mental energy;
he is therefore a laborer. A part of his income is wages, and this part is also
high on account of the great degree of skill required in the business. As he is
at the same time residual claimant, he is in the position of the entrepreneur,
and is entitled to any profit that may appear. The speculator, therefore,
combines the three functions of capitalist, laborer and entrepreneur.

ous industry, it must be willing to pay a price high enough to replace the capital accidentally destroyed as well as that used up in the process of production. Such replacement keeps the fund of capital intact, and so long as that is done, society as a whole is not concerned with the way in which the fortunes of individual capitalists may be affected by accidental causes. To the individual, however, it makes a great difference whether he is the one who suffers the accidental loss or the one who escapes. If his capital has been accidentally destroyed, it is small comfort to him to know that the social fund of capital has been kept intact. He is, therefore, reluctant to invest his capital in hazardous industries, and he does it only when the average net return in them is above the marginal return in safe investments. This extra net return which the investor demands on account of uncertainty is the reward for risk-taking. The amount of the reward will vary with the degree of the uncertainty. It will be fixed for each degree of risk by the reluctance of the marginal investor whose capital has to be employed under conditions where it is exposed to that risk.

Entrepreneurs have to pay for the capital they borrow in proportion to the risk to which it is to be exposed. To the entrepreneur, therefore, reward for risk-taking is a part of the expense of production. He recoups himself by adding the extra cost to the price of the commodity he produces. In this way the cost of risk is finally shifted to the consumers. Consumers, then, as well as capitalists, have a voice in determining whether a hazardous industry shall be carried on. The capitalist decides what net reward he will require on account of the uncertainty. The consumer then indicates whether his desire for the product of the industry is so intense that he is willing to pay a price for it which will replace the capital used up and accidentally destroyed and leave the capitalist the reward which he demands.

There are two ways in which society may reduce the cost of uncertainty. It may adopt means to prevent the occurrence of accidental loss, or measures which will reduce the degree of uncertainty or its repellent influence without affecting the amount of positive loss. All measures of the former kind may be grouped under the name of prevention. The advisability of adopting any such device depends upon the relative expense of production with it and without it. It is the entrepreneur who decides, and he does it by comparing the interest on the cost of the preventive measure with the saving of interest on his present investment through the diminution of risk. Those measures will be adopted which in the end are cheaper than the uncertainty they annihilate.

The general method of reducing uncertainty and unwillingness to bear it is through the transfer of risk. Considered as a transaction between individuals, this is advantageous to society whenever the one to whom the risk is transferred is for any reason less reluctant to carry it than the one from whom it is transferred. Its greatest benefit, however, is realized only when the risks of many individuals are combined in a group. When this is done the degree of uncertainty for the group as a whole is diminished. The risk of the group is less than the sum of the risks of the individuals. The institution through which this combination of risks is generally brought about is insurance.

Accumulations to meet accidental losses of capital are called insurance funds. As the amount of loss which will occur is in the nature of the case more or less uncertain, the amount of accumulation cannot be fixed exactly at the amount of loss. It is fixed at the probable amount of loss, as determined by past experience, with an allowance for fluctuations. This allowance varies with the degree of uncertainty as to the variation of the actual loss from the average. If all producers carry their own risks, the sum of these extra accumulations due to uncertainty will be very great. When the risks of the individuals are transferred to an insurance company, the company makes the accumulations for the entire group. Since the degree of uncertainty for the company is far less than that of any individual producer, the amount of the accumulation, when it is made by the company, is less than the sum of the accumulations of the individuals. The total accumulation is brought nearer to the total loss, and the extra amount, which from the point of view of society is an undesirable expense, is greatly reduced. Insurance is a method of making accumulations to meet uncertain losses, and the economic benefit which it confers upon society is the result of the reduction in the amount of these accumulations and the elimination of the part due to uncertainty.

The desire to secure the gain which the combination of risks produces is a force which fosters the growth of insurance. After the institution has once been introduced, it is evident that in the absence of opposing influences its use will become universal. If primary dynamic changes were to cease, when time had been allowed for all friction to be overcome and for the static adjustment of the productive forces of society to be reached, all forms of risk existing in such a society would be found combined in one group. The number of risks in such a group would be so great that the allowance to be made for fluctuations of losses would be almost or entirely eliminated. The amount of positive loss would not be affected, but the amount of the accumulation to meet the accidental loss would be fixed approximately at the amount of the loss. The individual producer, no longer feeling the necessity of protecting himself against disaster, would no longer feel any reluctance to enter an industry on account of risk. So far as the influence of risk was concerned, there would be that perfect static adjustment of capital which insures its greatest productivity, and the negative loss which unequal degrees of risk would cause in a static state would entirely disappear.